Schultz

Eldridge Cleaver

Eldridge Cleaver

POST-PRISON

WRITINGS AND

SPEECHES /

EDITED AND WITH

AN APPRAISAL BY

Robert Scheer

A *R*AMPARTS BOOK

RANDOM HOUSE / NEW YORK

Contents

INTRODUCTION

I last saw Eldridge Cleaver on a Sunday evening in San Francisco, three days before he was scheduled to turn himself in to the California Adult Authority for a *pro forma* hearing and subsequent shipment to prison. We had left the chaotic warmth of a Chinatown restaurant and were on the corner of Columbus and Pacific streets waiting for the light to change before crossing over for a cappuccino at La Tosca. Chatting about whether or not the Yenching's Princess Chicken was too spicy, we barely noticed the patrol car that slipped around the corner. It stopped suddenly and backed up, the tires squealing. The doors sprang open and two cops jumped out and headed toward Cleaver, hands on holsters, shouting, "What did you call us?" In the confusion, two other patrol cars had pulled up behind us, red lights flashing.

Back in the restaurant, Eldridge had tried patiently to explain to me that the guards would see to his death if he went back to prison and that the "pigs" had in fact been trying for the past year to provoke him and other Black Panther leaders into a final, apocalyptic shoot-out. While I have never been completely comfortable with the word "pig," there was no doubt about the men rushing toward us: their faces were flushed pink and uncomprehending, and suddenly "pig" seemed terribly precise. As they moved on Eldridge, I summoned the vestiges of middle-class respectability and began waving a clip of police press passes and credit cards at them. A sympathetic crowd had begun to listen to my ravings about police provocation and freedom of the press, and the "pigs" decided to become "officers" again. I was suddenly referred to as Mr. Scheer—and given the illogical admonishment, "Don't ask for police assistance the next time unless it is really required." They left.

Cleaver had remained immobile throughout the scene, barely visible against the night in his black trench coat. But he was going through changes, from a calm acceptance of the inevitable to open scorn and bitter laughter when the pigs left in reluctant tribute to my display of white power. He told me that had he been walking alone he would have been killed, and from what I had seen of those swollen police faces I knew he was right.

We forgot about the cappuccino, shook hands for the last time and Eldridge Cleaver, whose *Soul on Ice* had just made the *New York Times* list of the ten outstanding books of the year, slipped off alone and up against it. Three days later he failed to offer himself as an object for the rehabilitation services of the California penal system, instead choosing to become a fugitive, a hunted "criminal." "Just like any hoodlum," said California's assistant attorney general, proving once again America's inability to accept the category of political prisoner.

Cleaver's disappearance marked, almost to the day, the second anniversary of his release from Soledad Prison, where he had served nine years of a sentence of one to fourteen years for rape—a decidedly lower-class crime. If he had embezzled public funds, as had a former San Francisco assessor who occupied the neighboring cell, that "one to fourteen" would have meant a two-year sentence and then parole. Cleaver was kept in jail longer because he had a past, which began at the age of twelve with the theft of a bicycle. And it did not help that he was a Muslim minister in prison, and insisted on the same rights to practice his religion as were given to adherents of the more acceptable faiths.

Cleaver obtained parole only after his lawyer, Beverly Axelrod, smuggled some of his writings out of jail and their publication in *Ramparts* resulted in the support of "prominent" persons. Cleaver was offered a contract for a book by McGraw-Hill, and he was offered a job at *Ramparts*—in those days sufficiently close to its origins as a lay-Catholic literary quarterly to provide respectable cover. These he could show the authorities as proof of his capacity to sustain life and respectability on the outside.

While in jail, Cleaver had left the Black Muslims and organized a class in Afro-American history and culture, which appeared innocent enough, though it was actually based on the teachings of Malcolm X. He also concentrated on his own writings, mainly personal and autobiographical in nature.

The authorities felt safe in assuming that Cleaver,

once on the outside, would at worst become merely another angry black writer—of some importance, perhaps, to small literary circles, but no sort of serious threat. Being realistic men, the prison authorities do not take books seriously. (Cleaver's parole officer recently stated that he still hasn't got around to reading *Soul on Ice,* although he did catch a review of it on TV.) And being realistic men, the authorities knew that if Cleaver ever got out of hand, he could be whisked back into jail without so much as a court hearing, to serve the remainder of his sentence.

So Cleaver was released in response to the pressure of concerned and respectable citizens on the outside—those who had proved their loyalty to the system by refusing to steal bicycles when they were twelve; who had opted for the art of seduction or purchases, in preference to rape; and who had limited their avarice to acts not clearly banned by the criminal code.

Cleaver himself was sufficiently "rehabilitated" after nine years to have picked up some of the survival techniques of those who freed him. So much so that after his release from jail, he went out and bought a Volvo station wagon on time, paid his rent bill, opened a savings account, and made all the required visits to his parole officer.

In the beginning the parole authorities seemed content enough with Cleaver's behavior because he did not backslide into criminal activity. But they soon perceived that he might be into something far worse—politics.

Cleaver had left jail in a state of political anxiety. His faith in the Black Muslim movement was shattered by its failure to protect its own and to work out a serious program of black power, and by its split with Malcolm X. ("Black history began with Malcolm X," he had written while still in jail.) Cleaver concluded that the Muslim movement was dead and that "it would take a visit by Allah in person to revive it."

But Malcolm X's organizations, formed after his break with the Muslims, had died with him, and Cleaver was a lonely figure for the first few months of his freedom. He attempted to sort out the myriad movements of radical black America—movements that he described as an "archipelago of one-man showcase groups that plagued the black community with division." Along with some other writers he set up the Black House in San Francisco, which became the center of non-Establishment black culture in the Bay Area. He also worked on reviving Malcom X's Organization of Afro-American Unity, this time to be based in the San Francisco Bay Area—but this effort soon floundered.

In these first months outside, Cleaver found that the black community was suffering from a surfeit of militant talk without any commensurate program of action, and was attempting to camouflage this failure by emphasizing "cultural nationalism" rather than political revolution. He soon felt that the cultural nationalists' excessive emphasis on the roots and virtues of black culture obscured the essential fact that blacks formed an oppressed colony in the midst of white America. He frequently cited Frantz Fanon's point that black culture bore the marks of that oppression and that the black man could wrest his manhood from white society only through revolutionary political struggle—not through posturing, dress, or reviving African cultural roots. In a review of a work by Fanon, Cleaver noted approvingly: "What this book does is legitimize the revolutionary impulse to violence. It teaches colonial subjects that it is perfectly normal for them to want to rise up and cut off the heads of the slavemasters, that it is a way to achieve their manhood, and that they must oppose the oppressor in order to experience themselves as men."

Cleaver knew that many white readers would respond to such an idea with cries of "black racism," but he also knew that such a response would reflect the reader's error, not his. He was always quite specific in pointing out that power is not equally distributed throughout white society, though all whites are part of the dominant culture, and in varying degrees share its implicit racism. He frequently drew an analogy with the Algerian war, in which individual Frenchmen managed to break with French society and support the revolution, but only after overcoming the colonialist mentality which had been inculcated in them since birth.

To opt against the system is difficult, and Cleaver feels it would be an unlikely choice for most whites ("There's a little of George Wallace in every white American"), but it is nonetheless an alternative for the nonracist white. In the conclusion of "The Courage to Kill," he raises the essential question for white Americans: "Which side do you choose? Do you side with the oppressor or with the oppressed? The time for decision is upon you."

One may not like the choice Cleaver offers, but since he does offer it, one is forced to find some grounds other than "black racism" to criticize. It is the conduct of whites, not their skin color, that he condemns. Cleaver's critics should concede that what they really find objectionable are his basic notion of the need for black independence, and his assumption that black people in America form an oppressed colony; his speeches were always centered on these points.

This belief in the necessity of black political revolution, which dominated Cleaver's thoughts even in those first months of searching, was to find a natural outlet in the Black Panther Party that Huey Newton and Bobby Seale had founded across the bay in Oakland. In "The Courage to Kill," Cleaver provides a detailed description of his initial encounter with the Panthers. It would be difficult to overemphasize the importance to his writing of this period of association with the Panthers, particularly with Newton and Seale. Without the Panthers, Cleaver would undoubtedly have developed a much more personal, career-oriented, literary way of life. With the Panthers, he became a disciplined political revolutionary as well as a literary polemicist, although there was hardly any time for writing. He was engaged in his political work to the point of physical exhaustion—infinitely more involved with an incident on Oakland's San Pablo Avenue than with the galleys for his next article.

Had Cleaver not joined the Panthers, he would have had it made. In America it is possible to be angry and remain safe—in fact, anger is even desirable in a writer so long as it is diffuse and inactive; it can make him entertaining and therefore marketable. An angry writer can indulge in freedom of choice among the life styles available to literary figures: the cocktail circuit or seclusion, occasionally punching fellow writers or savoring nonviolence, being a writer-in-residence in Iowa or diddling with a dog in a car in Denver. The writer's "freedom" is permitted so long as what he says does not threaten the dominant society—so long as it is not coupled with action.

The Panthers began to be a threat when they started to pack guns—a right that white Californians had exercised ever since they had discovered the state away from the Indians and Mexicans. The Panthers proceeded to organize young blacks in the ghetto—the "brothers off the block," Bobby Seale calls them—into self-defense units, which patrolled the police; they also began to push a radical, ten-point program for black power, and to build alliances of support with white radicals. Cleaver, as Minister of Information of the Black Panther Party, placed his writing skills at the disposal of the Panthers, and as the party consolidated its power, he became a prime target of the California authorities' wrath.

Three months after his release, in February 1967, he began working covertly with Newton and Seale. But the parole authorities did not move against him for this early and tentative association with the Panthers, who were as yet a small group confined to the Oakland area and not much in the news. It was Cleaver's appearance as one of the main speakers at San Francisco's Kezar Stadium on April 15, 1967, before 65,000 Vietnam war protesters, that sounded the first real alarm with the parole authorities.

Mrs. Martin Luther King was the rally's featured speaker (her husband spoke at the same time, at the much larger counterpart demonstration in New York City). The importance of the event, along with the prominence accorded Cleaver's speech, made it occasion for an official reprimand.

A few days after the rally Cleaver was obliged to meet, at the *Ramparts* office, with his parole officer, a Mr. Bilideau, and with Bilideau's superior. The unusual presence of the second officer underscored the depth of the state's concern. I had been asked to attend in my capacity as managing editor of *Ramparts* because it was Cleaver's activities as a "public figure and writer" that were to be discussed. The parole officers were obviously embarrassed as they explained that the content of Cleaver's speech at the rally had been found offensive by Governor Reagan and members of the Adult Authority, the controlling body of the penal system in California, whose members are appointed by the governor. The parole officers stated most explicitly that Cleaver would not long remain "at large" if he repeated such speeches.

The speech in question had advocated the basic program of the Black Panther Party, including the call for black self-defense and identification of the black struggle with the one being waged by the National Liberation Front in Vietnam. The two officials stated that, in the future, they would have to approve the content of Cleaver's speeches in advance before granting him permission to speak. I noted that this censorship blatantly violated Cleaver's rights; they countered, with blunt simplicity, that a parolee "had no rights." If Governor Reagan didn't like Cleaver's behavior, he would put him back in prison.

The parole officers were there to argue not law but power, and Cleaver understood them much better than I. He stilled my bouncy indignation by dismissing them as "faceless men" caught up in a bureaucracy that owned them, mind and soul. Writing later about this incident, Cleaver said, ". . . they were organization men and experience had taught me that on receiving orders from above, they would snap into line and close ranks against me."

Cleaver informed his parole officer that while he was willing to play all the little parolee games, such as reporting four times each month and requesting permission to travel, he drew the line at submitting his speeches and/or writings for approval. They were forced to back down on the censorship issue after Cleaver's attorneys began to file briefs, but the basic scenario had been written: Cleaver would fight the state, and the state would try to break him.

Two weeks later Cleaver was arrested in Sacramento when a delegation of armed Black Panthers attempted to attend a legislative hearing on gun control. It was still legal then to carry guns in California; but not, according to a little-noticed law, in a state building. Cleaver was arrested a few blocks away with some of the Panthers who were driving back to San Francisco. A parole "Hold" was put on him and bail withheld. The cops who took him in gleefully informed him that he "had had it" and would never get out.

But it soon became clear that someone had made a mistake, for Cleaver's parole officer had previously granted him permission to be in Sacramento to cover the Panther action for *Ramparts*. It was demonstrated through TV footage that Eldridge held a camera rather than a gun, and was standing off with the press people during the encounter, rather than with the Panther contingent. The authorities released him, reluctantly; but they slapped on new restrictions, limiting his travel to San Francisco, with the Bay Bridge and Oakland off-limits. There were to be no speeches or appearances.

He was ordered not to say anything "critical of the California Department of Corrections or any California politician."

Cleaver decided to "play it cool and go along with them," challenging their decision in the courts while concentrating in the interim on writing and internal Panther organizing. The travel restriction was subsequently eased somewhat, and he was able to travel on *Ramparts* assignments when they were approved by the authorities. The official discretion to limit his movements was always exercised in a capricious manner. Frequently permission was refused, as it was when *Ramparts* wanted to send Cleaver to cover the Democratic and Republican conventions, although *Ramparts* had secured a press credential that would have admitted him to the conventions' press galleries.

This uneasy status quo, with Cleaver semi-active, continued until, the following October, Huey Newton was shot and arrested, in a confrontation with Oakland police in which one cop died. Bobby Seale, the party's Chairman, was already in jail on a charge stemming from the Sacramento incident. The Panthers were being harassed at every turn, and were in a poor position to mount a campaign of support for Newton. Cleaver recalled later, ". . . I was the only other effective public speaker that we had. . . . So in November I started making speeches again and writing in Huey's defense. . . . Helping Huey stay out of the gas chamber was more important than my staying out of San Quentin."

In the following month the Panthers formed an alliance with the Peace and Freedom Party that eventually resulted in Cleaver's candidacy for President and Newton's for Congress. Cleaver's renewed public speaking made him a prime target, once again, for the police, who were bent on destroying the Panthers. His picture came to be used as a dartboard in police stations, supplementing Newton's. He was regularly tailed and harassed by the cops.

On January 15, 1968, at 3 A.M., members of the Special Tactical Squad of the San Francisco Police Department forced their way into the Cleaver residence and held Cleaver and his wife at gunpoint while they looked for something incriminating to book him on. They didn't find anything, and this proved to be their last chance for the more obvious type of frame-up, for in the following month Cleaver's book *Soul on Ice* was published and he became nationally known through reviews and TV appearances. The police now required a more dramatic incident if they were to return Cleaver to prison without generating excessive public support on his behalf.

On April 6, two days after Martin Luther King was killed, Cleaver was in the *Ramparts* office in the late afternoon, dictating his article, "Requiem For Nonviolence." In a matter of hours he and other Panthers came to be involved in a shoot-out with the Oakland police. Seventeen-year-old Bobby Hutton died, shot in the back moments after he and Eldridge, arms above their heads, stumbled out from the building where they had taken refuge. Cleaver, who was wounded in the leg, was first taken to Oakland's Highland Hospital; then to the Alameda County Courthouse where the police made him lie on the floor while he was being booked; and finally, that same night, to San Quentin Hospital where a guard pushed him down a flight of stairs. He was brought to the State Medical Facility at Vacaville and confined in the "hole." After hearing the first radio report, I had gone down to Highland in time to see Cleaver being hustled out under the shotguns of no fewer than twelve Oakland cops. His eyes were so swollen from tear gas that he could barely make it into the ambulance, but the cops kept their fingers on the triggers, quite obviously more in hopeful anticipation of an excuse to fire than in concern for their own safety.

His parole was quickly revoked, and for two months he sat at Vacaville. The Adult Authority had exercised its power to suspend or revoke parole without notice or hearing, basing its action solely on the police reports. Three parole violations were listed: possession of firearms, associating with individuals of bad reputation, and failing to cooperate with the parole agent. The Adult Authority studied Cleaver's parole record for other possible violations to beef up its case, but could produce only one—the claim that he had failed to report in after returning from an authorized trip to New York to tape the David Susskind show.

Cleaver's attorney, Charles Garry, petitioned for a writ of habeas corpus in the court of Superior Court Judge Raymond J. Sherwin in Solano County, which includes Vacaville. Amazingly, after a hearing the writ was granted. Cleaver admitted later that he was confounded by the fact that a white judge in a small rural county in California had acted impartially.

Dismissing the charge of association with individuals of bad reputation, Judge Sherwin noted that the Adult Authority had not even bothered to identify them as individuals: "None was further identified except as members of the Black Panther Party . . . two or three of those named had 'police records' but nothing to show whether any had been convicted of anything, or whether Cleaver knew of their arrest records." As for the charge of noncooperation with his parole officer, the judge noted that, in fact, "Cleaver did report by telephone the day after his return from New York." And on the possession of firearms charge, the judge stated: "Cleaver's only handling of a firearm [the rifle] was in obedience to a police command. He did not handle a hand gun at all. There was nothing one way or the other to show a conspiracy or a situation calling for the application of the doctrine of aiding and abetting. Hence, nothing supported either the possession of a firearm or the assault charges."

Judge Sherwin went on to observe:

> The record here is that though the petitioner was arrested and his parole cancelled more than two months ago, hearings before the Adult Authority have not even been scheduled. There is nothing to indicate why it was deemed necessary to cancel his parole before his trial on the pending of criminal charges of which he is presumed innocent.

This decision to grant Cleaver the writ of habeas corpus was all the more remarkable in that it moved beyond the technical legal arguments to confront directly the political basis for the harassment:

> It has to be stressed that the uncontradicted evidence presented to this Court indicated that the petitioner had been a model parolee. The peril to his parole status stemmed from no failure of per-

sonal rehabilitation, but from his undue eloquence in pursuing political goals, goals which were offensive to many of his contemporaries. Not only was there absence of cause for the cancellation of parole, it was the product of a type of pressure unbecoming, to say the least, to the law enforcement paraphernalia of this State.

The law-enforcement paraphernalia was not at all intimidated by the Superior Court judge's strictures, and the Adult Authority moved immediately to have his ruling reversed in the Appellate Court. In the interim, Sherwin's writ allowed for Cleaver's release on the $50,000 bail that had been set.

The Appellate Court behaved more predictably than Judge Sherwin had—it was true to the power arrangement that obtains in California. The court refused to examine the facts at issue in the case and instead simply affirmed the arbitrary power of the Adult Authority to revoke parole. The governor appoints court judges as well as the members of the Adult Authority, and it was not unexpected that the State Supreme Court agreed with the Appellate Court. Both courts of course refused to consider the political issues involved, assuming—as is the custom—the political neutrality of the Oakland cops and Reagan's Adult Authority. So Cleaver was scheduled to be returned to jail in sixty days, on November 27, and it is his failure to keep this date that has resulted in his status as a fugitive.

When he was released on bail, Cleaver said that the two months he had spent in Vacaville were "harder time" than his previous nine-year stretch, for he had found himself and tasted freedom in the interim in the outside world. Perhaps because of the tension of those two months in Vacaville, or because of his feeling of debit for Bobby Hutton's death when he himself had been the target, Cleaver came out of Vacaville determined to confront white California from Ronald Reagan on down. Cleaver was possessed, and the words came as readily as the invitations to speak. He ran for President on the ticket of the Peace and Freedom Party, which had, whatever its other failings, managed the incredible feat of getting over one hundred thousand Californians to register into a new radical party and secure it a place on the ballot. He consistently pushed the issue of Huey Newton into public view, and there was a limited victory when Newton was convicted on manslaughter instead of the first-degree murder verdict sought by the D.A. ("In Oakland yet! That Charles Garry's so bad, he's the first white panther," Cleaver said.) Then an invitation came to teach in an experimental sociology course at the University of California at Berkeley in the fall of 1968. The course dealt with the problem of racism, and the Oakland police chief and others had agreed to be participants along with Cleaver. A few Berkeley radicals warned Cleaver not to teach the course, so he wouldn't be co-opted by the system. But he knew that the issue was perfect. The Academic Senate had approved the creation of the course, and they had traditionally been granted power over the design or establishment of courses. But the University of California Regents, at Ronald Reagan's instigation, attempted to block the course, thus acting in violation of established procedures.

As the U.C. issue splattered across California newspapers, Cleaver moved up and down the state from Humboldt to Orange County, "roasting Reagan's tail" in a series of public addresses. Campus liberals and radicals were for once united on an issue, and the TV and newspaper coverage of the duel between the Sanctimonious Reagan and Freeswinging Cleaver was fantastic. Cleaver played the media. It was power, and he respected it; at the same time, he never catered to it. His performance was one-man guerrilla theater with all the baddies uptight, and kids and other good types loving it.

Eldridge Cleaver had somehow managed to insert himself between Ronald Reagan and the liberal community. The Regents had given Cleaver the issue that made him the focal point of anti-Reagan feeling whatever its source—the New Left *enragés,* the hippies, the blacks, or the white liberals. He alone had managed to drag Reagan out there to do battle, "away from the script that they had carefully constructed" for him, as Cleaver gleefully described it. It was a wild romp through what Eldridge called Mad Babylon (his term for White America), and it became intolerable to the men who run the state. Throughout the whole affair, Cleaver's every action denied the legitimacy of their power. And Cleaver's irreverence was particularly confounding because his analysis of the times had the ring of truth.

He spoke out front during these always-extemporaneous speeches. He proved an uneven, though at times brilliant speaker. As he spoke, he moved around his subject, darting in and out until he had uncovered some key points, and then he poured it on. When it didn't happen, when he hadn't got hold of the essential truth, then the pouring on didn't help—the invective or obscenity was sour and Cleaver knew it, and his mind turned for relief to less serious, though perhaps more bizarre, comments.

During that period we flew down together to Orange County, the Mecca of California's resurgent Right Wing, to share a panel at the University of California at Irvine, not far from Disneyland and Knotts' Berry Farm. There had been dozens of threats on his life from the local citizenry, and the Santa Ana *Register* had carried blazing headlines about "Cleaver Death Threats," which were displayed to us by the stewardess as we were about to land. The local sheriff's deputies were at the airport in force in their cowboy hats, and the head man came up, shook Cleaver's hand, and assured him that they would do the best they could. Cleaver burst out laughing, "You're the sheriff of *what?*" And when it had registered that the thirty-odd deputies were "protection" rather than a lynch mob, Cleaver, very solemnly and in the time-honored tradition of presidential candidates, proceeded to salute each one, adding "Right on" for encouragement.

The audience at the college was made up of children of the people who run Orange County. They had stiffly assumed the very correct posture of defending to the death Cleaver's right to speak; but they would go no further. Cleaver caught their mood and tried very patiently to explain the facts of his case, what Reagan had said, and what the Regents had declared. It was all getting terribly complicated and detailed when Cleaver cut through by asking, "Who the hell is Mickey Mouse Ronald Reagan to tell you who you can hear, to tell me when I can speak and to tell the faculty how many lectures of mine they can schedule—to all that I can only say Fuck Reagan." They weren't so much shocked as caught. It wasn't the word "fuck," which is, if anything, feeble from overuse, but rather the idea that "Fuck Reagan" might just be the necessary response to the elaborate edifice of hypocrisy that had been built up around his governorship. The crowd gasped for a very long ten seconds and then, very timidly, began to applaud. Applause became a liberating act, building into a nearly unanimous three-minute ovation. Cleaver had got across.

I have never found anyone, white or black, who has met Cleaver and not been enormously impressed. A *Saturday Evening Post* article said about him, "He is the only genuinely militant black extremist in the public eye today who deeply and honestly likes white men, and believes the two races can get along and work together for the good of everyone." Cleaver, like Huey Newton and Bobby Seale, is a committed black revolutionary, and whites who side with the oppressive mother country are enemies to be dealt with "by any means necessary," but he has followed their lead in drawing that distinction—so beautifully developed by the Vietnamese revolutionaries—between the people in the mother country and those who manipulate and use them. He was less alienated from white audiences than are most white radical speakers, and he always managed to get his subject around to some basic human level through ironic humor, reference to love, or a cold dissection of the lies and liars.

The Reagan-Cleaver duel that Eldridge called for in his "Aside to Ronald Reagan" actually did take place in California during those fall months, and the results were so comically disastrous to what Cleaver calls the "punks with power" that they moved to call time on the game. The Reagan administration became frantic in its obvious desire to get Cleaver back to jail. Cleaver never doubted that, at this stage at least, they held the cards, but he was going to make it as tough for them as possible—and surrenderingly meekly on that November 27 was not his idea of how best to make it tough.

He has stated frequently that he is more than willing to stand trial because the evidence is so clear that even in an Oakland court, he would be able to prove his innocence, and prove the guilt of the Oakland cops in the murder of Bobby Hutton. In any event, that information will come out in the trial of the other four defendants. But Cleaver felt certain that no matter what the outcome of the trial, they would try to kill him in jail (an easy matter to arrange through one of the convicts) or keep him there for life. Otherwise, he reasoned, why are they so bent on putting me in jail on parole violation only weeks before the trial?

He confided to audiences that he was too taken with a freedom that he had not known before to be confident of surviving jail. When Cleaver had first come out, he had looked ill at ease in large rooms or on the street, and seemed always to prefer the closeness of his small writing cubicle at *Ramparts*. He was wary in conversation and seemed to tense up like a street fighter almost instinctively, even when there was nothing more threatening in sight than a British secretary. But Cleaver took easily to freedom and women and food and Scotch and Berkeley and Bobby Dylan and the soul food near the Panther office. He came to embody a good chunk of the black, bohemian, student and radical worlds that thrive in the Bay Area. He came to love it so much to be outside, among swarms of people—at Yippie be-ins, Panther park rallies or the Monterey Jazz Festival—that when he thought he was dying in the Oakland shoot-out he recalls that he bathed himself in images of crowds:

> . . . my mind seemed to dwell on crowds of people, masses of people, millions of people . . . I remembered the people at the rally in the Oakland Auditorium, the surging, twisting sea of people at the Peace and Freedom Party Convention . . .

All political leaders use crowds—exploit their collective energy and vitality. Most politicians simply manipulate crowds, to serve their own egos. Cleaver was among the few who could draw on the crowd's strength and then feed the strength back again. That requires taking chances, thinking out loud; there is the risk of sounding dumb, but that's a lesser sin than being distant. In those last months Cleaver got so high on the people he met, and he gave out so much, that he entered a rare dimension of freedom—even if they didn't manage to actually kill him in prison, Cleaver could never again live in captivity.

The hyperactivity of the last months of speaking tours prevented Cleaver from doing much writing other than the brief "Aside to Ronald Reagan." For that reason the Stanford speech has been included in this collection as illustrative of his thoughts in that period. But he did take time out for one writing project: the biography of Huey Newton as dictated by Bobby Seale, parts of which were published in *Ramparts*. Cleaver seemed obsessed with this project for two reasons: he has an historian's sense of social movement, and he was determined to record precisely the events that contributed to the development of the Panthers. But there was also the matter of Huey Newton's importance to Cleaver's own development, which has been completely overlooked by those who have written about Eldridge. In his introduction to Seale's work, Cleaver wrote: "Having myself joined the Black Panther Party, and accepted Huey P. Newton as my leader, I find myself sharing with Bobby Seale the same attitude towards Huey—the same willingness to place my life in his hands . . ." Cleaver acknowledged the difference between Huey's style and his own, but respected both. What he seems to admire most in Huey Newton is his sense of sustained purpose, his preoccupation with the long haul and his deadly serious and ordered commitment. Eldridge, despite his own occasional half-hearted efforts to the contrary, is very much the impulsive, lusty, bohemian writer. He thrives in chaos.

Cleaver liked the action that was his through writing and speaking. But he consistently tried to direct the media's attention away to what he claimed were more serious subjects: Newton's ideas, and the program of the Black Panther Party. The biography of Huey Newton was one way of doing that, and he demonstrated a studiousness on this project that he had not been able to devote to his own recent writings, which were always done against the last possible deadline. Some, like the smaller pieces printed in this collection, are actually newspaper columns, none of which took more than thirty minutes to execute. But the biography was "history" as well as "literature," and he lavished his time on the project.

Cleaver's politics so dominated his two years of freedom that his printed works must be judged as polemics, with the critical stress placed upon the concepts advanced rather than on literary style. He wrote these pieces to meet specific political problems; they were written on the run.

This collection, then, is not a sequel to *Soul on Ice,* which was written during the leisure of Cleaver's forced confinement. In this book one finds the art of the journalist, and in that sense it is a first book. Comparisons with *Soul on Ice* will inevitably be made by reviewers, but Cleaver was not in a position to work on assembling this book, as he was with the other, and he bears no responsibility for the particular selections, which are almost entirely from *Ramparts* and were drawn together while he was a fugitive unavailable for consultation. This book has not drawn upon his very substantial number of speeches or his articles for the Black Panther newspaper and other publications. It was rushed through production in order to answer the need of people to come to grips with Cleaver's political ideas— which evolved through contact with the outside world and hence are in the post-*Soul on Ice* period—and because the media which have made so much of his name have largely ignored his ideas. But there is a more pressing need for this book: Cleaver is now the subject of white America's wrath—he has been given the choice of flight or death in prison.

The intellectual and liberal community in America, which is normally agitated by violations of the rights of Soviet artists, has displayed monumental indifference to the most harassed and promising of its own young writers. That host of organizations, PEN, the Congress of Cultural Freedom, International Rescue Committee and other "free world" crusaders normally charged with the protection of liberty against totalitarian regimes, seem constitutionally incapable of finding analogous problems in this country. *Newsweek* magazine was terribly agitated about the imprisonment of Soviet writer Daniel, but found Cleaver's plight a source of amusement—"soul on the lam"—and at last report *The Saturday Review* had not yet been heard from, nor had Norman Podhoretz.

Perhaps these folk are interested only in preserving freedom for ideas that are not threatening to them. But what about the rest of us? What does it say about our lives that we can function here as writers, editors, citizens, but that Eldridge Cleaver cannot?

One almost feels that it is in poor taste to raise that matter of the line which forces us to take a side, but it does after all exist, and Eldridge Cleaver's writings stand against obscuring it. Cleaver is now a fugitive because of his ideas. The legal charges against him are the sort of drivel one finds in these cases anywhere in the world. He has been forced out of American society simply through the vindictiveness of the Adult Authority of the State of California, which wanted him hustled off to jail before his trial in Oakland. No matter what the judgment of the jury, the Adult Authority held total power over Cleaver's freedom.

The California courts, with the exception of Judge

Sherwin, had refused to even consider the facts in his case, and when U.S. Supreme Court Justice Thurgood Marshall turned down a last-minute appeal for a stay, Cleaver left.

It was not unexpected that the Panthers would be unwilling to put another one of their leaders in the hands of the California Adult Authority. His fate would be no better than that of Huey Newton, who is kept under such close scrutiny that it is not possible for him to communicate his political thoughts either through interviews or in writing. Cleaver could not accept that silence.

The "faceless" men of the Adult Authority have acted for us; we should know them better. Five of the eight members of the Authority were appointed by Ronald Reagan. Its chairman, Henry Kerr, was second in command of the Los Angeles police force during its most racist period. The vice-chairman, Curtis O. Lynum, was chief special agent in charge of the San Francisco FBI; another member was the former commander of the Narcotics Division of the L.A. Police Department; one was a career prison official; and yet another was the deputy district attorney in Los Angeles County.

It's as unsavory a group as has ever moved against a revolutionary writer, but what is most incredible is that the rest of us seem prepared to accept the inevitability of its power.

We have come to rely on a numbing appeal to "realism" as an alternative to confronting the fact that America has an enormous number of political prisoners—from white draft resisters to Black Panthers—and the fact that those of us on the outside are permitted our freedom on the supposition that we do not follow their path, that we do not seriously trouble the status quo of power.

Cleaver was particularly troubling because he was outrageously public, perhaps the most upfront man alive. He confounded his critics by using their own institutions to demonstrate their insignificance, from running for President to teaching a course at "Cal." And he managed to put whites on the spot—to draw that line more clearly than any other black leader. It was his job to run down what he called "the cold shit."

There really was a little old lady in Orange County who sent Eldridge a note about his language: "I like what you're saying, Mr. Cleaver, but your bad words hurt my ears." He told her "Right on, lady," welcoming her to the revolution, and hung her note on his office wall. But he still needed the words. "It's not that I don't know a few other words—it's just that I feel that most of the things that are going on in this country no longer need analyzing. The shit has been analyzed and talked about from side to side, for decades and generations." He continued, to the young lawyers in the San Francisco Barristers' Club: "What we're saying today is that you're either part of the solution or you're part of the problem. There is no middle ground . . . Because those in the middle, those who are standing on the side, watching these pigs brutalize people, they see the boot on a man's neck and they're going to stand there, and try to decide who to help. . . . All of you pigs who want to support the other side, just fuck you, pig, and I hope that some nigger catches you on a dark street and kills you. . . . All of those who are not going to choose that side, I love you. And I recognize your humanity and I hope that you can recognize mine."

Right on, Eldridge.

ROBERT SCHEER

December 17, 1968

Eldridge Cleaver

AFFIDAVIT #1
I AM 33 YEARS OLD

In the aftermath of the Oakland shoot-out Cleaver's parole was revoked and he was sent to Vacaville Prison. While there, he prepared the following affidavit as a document to be used in his legal defense.

I am thirty-three years old. My first fifteen years were given to learning how to cope with the world and developing my approach to life. I blundered in my choices and set off down a road that was a dead end. Long years of incarceration is what I found on that road, from Juvenile Hall at the beginning to San Quentin, Folsom, and Soledad State Prisons at the end. From my sixteenth year, I spent the next fifteen years in and out of prison, the last time being an unbroken stay of nine years.

During my last stay in prison, I made the desperate decision to abandon completely the criminal path and to redirect my life. While in prison, I concentrated on developing the skills of a writer and I wrote a book which a publisher bought while I was still in prison and which was published after I was out on parole.

It looked like smooth sailing for me. I had fallen in love with a beautiful girl and got married; my book was soon to be published, and I had a good job as a staff writer with *Ramparts* magazine in San Francisco. I had broken completely with my old life. Having gone to jail each time out of Los Angeles, I had also put Los Angeles behind me, taking my parole to the Bay Area. I had a totally new set of friends and, indeed, I had a brand new life.

The thought of indulging in any "criminal activity" was as absurd and irrelevant as the thought of sprouting wings and flying to the moon. Besides, I was too busy. I joined the Black Panther Party, and because of my writing skills and interest in communications, became the editor of the party's newspaper, *The Black Panther*. In this I found harmony with my wife, Kathleen, who had worked in the communications department of SNCC in Atlanta, Georgia, and who, after our marriage, moved to San Francisco, joined the Black Panther Party, and became our Communications Secretary. Also, she is our party's candidate for the 18th Assembly District seat in San Francisco, running on the Peace and Freedom Party ticket. With my job at *Ramparts*, my political activity, editing the newspaper, and work on a new book, I had more to do than I could handle. My life was an endless round of speeches, organizational meetings, and a few hours snatched here and there on my typewriter.

I thought that the parole authorities would be pleased with my new life because in terms of complying with the rules governing conduct on parole, I was a model parolee. But such was not the case. My case was designated a "Special Study Case," which required that I see my parole agent four times each month, once at home, once at my job, once "in the field," and once in his office. My parole agent, Mr. R. L. Bilideau, was white, but his boss, Mr. Isaac Rivers, was a black man. Together these two gentlemen were my contact with the parole authorities. On a personal level, we got along very well together, and we spent many moments talking about the world and its problems. However, I could never believe in them as sincere friends, because they were organization men and experience had taught me that, on receiving orders from above, they would snap into line and close ranks against me.

The first time this happened was when, on April 15, 1967, I made a speech at Kezar Stadium criticizing this country's role in the war in Vietnam. The speech was part of the program of the Spring Mobilization Against the War in Vietnam, during the International Days of Protest. There were demonstrations from coast to coast. Dr. Martin Luther King spoke at the rally in New York and his wife at our rally at Kezar. The crowd was estimated at about 65,000 and the speeches were shown on television. Members of the parole authority, who don't like me, I was told, saw excerpts of my speech on TV and launched their campaign to have my parole revoked, but failed. Even though I had a perfect right to free speech, Mr. Rivers and Mr. Bilideau said there were those in the State Capital who, for political purposes, were clamoring to have my parole revoked and me returned to prison. They advised me to cool it and forsake my rights in the interest of not antagonizing those in Sacramento who did not like my politics. From then on, I was under constant pressure through them to keep my mouth shut and my pen still on any subject that might arouse a negative reaction in certain circles in Sacramento. Because I was violating neither any law of the land nor any rule of parole, upon being assured by my attorney that I was strictly within my rights, I decided not to accept these warnings and continued exercising my right to free speech and to write what was on my mind.

The next crisis occurred two weeks later when I was arrested in Sacramento with a delegation of armed Black Panthers, who visited the Capitol in this manner as a shrewd political and publicity gesture. The news media, heavily concentrated in the Capitol, gave the Black Panthers a million dollars' worth of publicity and helped spread the Panther message to black people that they should arm themselves against a racist country that was becoming increasingly repressive. Although I was there as a reporter, with an assignment from my magazine, and with the advance permission of my parole agent, I was arrested by the Sacramento police; and then the parole authority slapped a "Hold" on me so that I could not get out on bail. To the surprise of both the cops and the parole authority, their investigations proved that my press credentials were in order, that I was indeed there on an assignment, and that I had permission from my parole agent—also, that I had been armed with nothing more lethal than a camera and a ball point pen. Still the Sacramento cops would not drop the charges and the parole authority would not lift its "Hold" until the judge, citing the obvious "mistake" on the part of the cops, released me on my own recognizance. Then, magnanimously, the parole authority lifted its "Hold."

When I returned to San Francisco, I was again told

about the clamor in Sacramento to have my parole revoked. My enemies, I was told, had stayed up all night scanning TV film footage, trying to find a shot of me with a gun in my hands. No luck. But anyhow, severe new restrictions were to be imposed. 1) I was not to go outside a seven mile area; specifically, I was not to cross the Bay Bridge. 2) I was to keep my name out of the news for the next six months; specifically, my face was not to appear on any TV screen. 3) I was not to make any more speeches. 4) And I was not to write anything critical of the California Department of Corrections or any California politician. In short, I was to play dead, or I would be sent back to prison. "All that Governor Reagan has to do," I was told, "is sign his name on a dotted line and you are dead, with no appeal." Knowing that this was true and with my back thus to the wall, I decided to play it cool and go along with them, as I didn't see what else I could do. My attorneys said that we could challenge it in court, but that I would probably have to pound the Big Yard in San Quentin for a couple of years, waiting for the court to hand down a decision. I was in a bad bag.

Things stayed like that, but after a couple of months the travel ban was lifted with all the other restrictions remaining in force.

Then, on October 28, 1967, Huey Newton, Minister of Defense and leader of our party, was shot down in the streets by an Oakland cop and was arrested and charged with the murder of one Oakland cop and the wounding of another. Bobby Seale, Chairman of our party, was serving a six months' jail sentence for the Sacramento incident, and I was the only other effective public speaker that we had. A campaign to mobilize support in Huey's defense had to be launched immediately. So in November, 1967, I started making speeches again and writing in Huey's defense. The political nature of the case, and the fact that it involved a frame-up by the Oakland Police Department and the D.A.'s office, dictated that I had not only to criticize politicians but also the police. Well, helping Huey stay out of the gas chamber was more important than my staying out of San Quentin, so I went for broke. TV, radio, newspapers, magazines, the works. I missed no opportunity to speak out with Huey's side of the story. Mr. Rivers and Mr. Bilideau told me that the decision had already been made above to revoke my parole at the first pretext. Living thus on borrowed time, I tried to get as much done as I possibly could before time ran out.

In the latter part of December, 1967, Bobby Seale's sentence ran out and he was free to speak. Mass public support for Huey had developed. Our party had formed a coalition with the new Peace and Freedom Party, demanding that Huey be set free. In addition, we arranged to run Huey for Congress in the 7th Congressional District of Alameda County, to run Bobby Seale for the 17th Assembly District, and, as I have mentioned, to run my wife, Kathleen, for the 18th Assembly seat in San Francisco.

With such a forum and with the assurance that we had already stimulated overwhelming support for Huey, I decided to back up a little. Maybe it was possible to stay the hand of the parole authority. I cut back drastically on my public speaking.

In January, the Police departments of Oakland, Berkeley and San Francisco unleashed a terror and arrest campaign against the Black Panther Party. Members of the party were being arrested and harassed constantly. On January 15, 1968, at 3 A.M. the Special Tactical Squad of San Francisco's Police Department kicked down the door of my home, terrorizing my wife, myself, and our party's Revolutionary Artist, Emory Douglass, who was our guest that night.

On February 17, which was Huey Newton's twenty-sixth birthday, we staged a huge rally at the Oakland Auditorium, featuring Stokely Carmichael and his first public speech following his triumphal tour of the revolutionary countries of the world, and also featuring, as a surprise guest, H. Rap Brown, along with the venerable James Foreman, who took the occasion to announce the merger of SNCC and the Black Panther Party. Held in the shadow of the Alameda County jail wherein Huey is confined, the theme of the rally was "Come See About Huey." Over five thousand people showed up, a shattering and unequivocal demonstration of the broad support built up for the Minister of Defense. A similar rally was held in Los Angeles the next day, and altogether Stokely spent nine days in California beating the drums for Huey.

Every time we turned around Bobby Seale was getting arrested on frivolous, trumped-up charges. On February 22, 1968, a posse of Berkeley police kicked down Bobby's door, dragging him and his wife, Artie, from bed and arresting them on a sensational charge of conspiracy to commit murder. The same night, six other members of the party were arrested on the same charge. The ridiculous charge of conspiracy to commit murder was quickly dropped, but all arrested were held to answer on various gun law violations, all of which were unfounded. All in all, during that hectic week, sixteen members of our party were arrested gratuitously and charged with offenses that had never been committed. Although we know that we will ultimately beat all of these cases in court, they constitute a serious drain on our time, energy, and financial resources, the last of which have always been virtually non-existent.

During these hectic days, public sentiment throughout the Bay Area swung heavily in our favor because it was obvious to a blind man that we were being openly persecuted by the police.

In the midst of all this, McGraw-Hill Publishing Co., on February 28, 1968, published my book, *Soul On Ice,* and a lot of publicity was focussed on me as a result. By this time, my parole agent had virtually given up coming to see me, sending for me, or even calling me on the phone, a development that kept my nerves on edge. Was this the calm before the storm?

I was out of the state most of the month of March, filling TV appearances with my book, mostly in New York.

On April 3, 1968, the Oakland Police Department invaded the regular meeting of our party at St. Augustine's Church at 27th and West Street. Led by a captain, brandishing shotguns, and accompanied by a white monsignor and a black preacher, about a dozen of them burst through the door. Neither Bobby Seale nor myself was at that particular meeting (Bobby was in L.A. and I had left minutes before the raid in response to an urgent call). Our National Captain, David Hilliard, was in charge. David said that the cops came in with their shotguns leveled, but that when they saw him in charge they looked confused and disappointed. Mumbling incoherently, they lowered their weapons and stalked out.

Father Neil, whose church it is, happened to be present to witness the entire event. Theretofore, criticism of the police had been just that, and although he was inclined to believe that there was some validity to all the complaints, it was all still pretty abstract to him because he had never witnessed anything with his own eyes. Well, he had witnessed it now, and in his own church—with ugly shotguns thrown down on innocent, unarmed people who were holding a quiet peaceful assembly. Father Neil was outraged. He called a press conference next day at which he denounced the Oakland Police Department for behaving like Nazi storm troopers inside his church. However, Father Neil's press conference was upstaged by the fact that earlier in the day, his brother of the cloth, Martin Luther King, had got assassinated in Memphis, Tennessee. An ugly cloud boding evil settled over the nation.

A few days prior to the assassination of Martin Luther King, Marlon Brando had flown up from Hollywood to find out for himself what the hell was going on in the Bay Area. We took him to my pad and talked and argued with him all night long, explaining to him our side of the story. We had to wade through the history of the world before everything was placed in perspective and Brando could see where the Black Panther Party was coming from. When Brando split back to Hollywood, after accompanying Bobby Seale to court next day, we felt that we had gained a sincere friend and valuable ally in the struggle.

On the third night following the raid on St. Augustine's church, members of the Oakland Police Department tried to kill me. They did kill my companion, Little Bobby Hutton, Treasurer of our party and the first Black Panther recruited by Huey Newton and

Bobby Seale when they organized the party in October, 1966. They murdered Little Bobby in cold blood. I saw them shoot him, with fifty guns aimed at my head. I did get shot in the leg.

I am convinced that I was marked for death that night, and the only reason I was not killed was that there were too many beautiful black people crowded around demanding that the cops not shoot me, too many witnesses for even the brazen, contemptuous and contemptible Oakland Pigs.

A few hours later at 4 A.M. on April 7, someone somewhere in the shadowy secret world of the California Adult Authority ordered my parole revoked. While I was still in the emergency ward of Highland Hospital, three Oakland cops kept saying to me: "You're going home to San Quentin tonight!" Before the sun rose on a new day, charged with attempted murder after watching Little Bobby being murdered and almost joining him, I was shackled hand and foot and taken by Lieutenant Snellgrove and two other employees of the Department of Corrections to San Quentin.

Lieutenant Snellgrove, whom I knew very well from my stay at San Quentin and who remembered me, looked at me and said, while we rode in the back seat of the car headed for San Quentin, "Bad night, huh?" He was not being facetious—what else could he say—and neither was I. "Yeah," I said. "About the baddest yet."

Further, Affiant sayeth not.

April 19, 1968

THE DECLINE OF
THE BLACK MUSLIMS

There was a time when the names Black Muslims and Elijah Muhammad were enough to start prison officials reaching for headache pills. Every black inmate's thoughts centered on the question of whether or not to convert to the Nation of Islam. For the white inmates this was a dark bag, which they peered into only to plot a defense against what they perceived as an imminent threat to their survival.

In those days if you walked into any prison in the State of California and visited the unit set aside for solitary confinement, there was absolutely no doubt that you'd find ten or fifteen Black Muslims who were being "disciplined" for staunchly confronting prison officials with implacable demands that Muslims be allowed to practice their religion with the same freedom and privileges as the Catholics, Jews, and Protestants.

Soledad, San Quentin, and Folsom were the prisons with the highest concentration of adherents to Islam. Because prison officials would not allow Muslim ministers to come in from outside to hold services as the ministers of other religions did, the Muslims in each pris-

on had organized themselves into a Mosque, with a hierarchy patterned rigidly after the structure of the
Mosques in the outside world. Each prison had its inmate minister, captain, and Fruit of Islam. Prison officials knew this, but all they could do was periodically
bundle up the leaders of each Mosque and transfer them
to another prison, or place them in solitary confinement
so that they could not communicate with the other
members of the Mosque. Through this means they were
always able to keep the Muslims off balance with the
task of constantly reorganizing their Mosques.

Even so, the Muslims were able to carry out a systematic program of proselytizing among the great pool
of potential converts found in every prison. During his
stay in prison, every black inmate was exposed to the
Black Muslims' teachings, and had to decide whether or
not to join. During the exercise periods, it was not a
rare sight to see several Muslims walking around the
yard, each with a potential convert to whom he would
be explaining the Message to the Black Man as taught
by Elijah Muhammad.

Now all that has changed, and it is easy to see that the
light which once shone so brightly has dimmed, if not
gone completely out, and the Muslims are no longer
taken seriously by the prison officials, other inmates, or
even by themselves. They no longer burn with the zeal
of a growing sect that has ambitions and hopes of becoming a dominant force in the environment.

The reasons for this are several and complex. The
most obvious cause of the decline of the Black Muslims
in prisons is that Allah has failed to come. In this sense,
the Muslims have fallen victim to their own predictions
of doom for the white devils. In order to prod the re-

luctant potential converts into a speedy decision on whether or not to join, the Muslims used to spread the word that Allah would destroy North America "next year" and that only those blacks who were already members of the Nation of Islam would be saved. If you wait much longer, they taught, you just might find yourself roasting in the flames along with the exiled demons of Europa. But the years passed and Allah never made the scene.

The second major reason for the decline of the Muslims in prisons was the split in the Nation of Islam that developed over the callous ouster and subsequent murder of Malcolm X, who was the universal hero of black prisoners. Malcolm died at the hands of assassins dispatched from some dark corner of the kingdom of this world. But the onus of his death rests squarely on the shoulders of Elijah Muhammad and the princes of the Nation of Islam in the upper echelons of the hierarchy. There is no doubt that they engineered his ouster from power over the New York Mosque, which he had built up from the ground.

To have paid out so coldly one who had worked so hotly to get the Nation over the hump brought about a doom in confidence and turned every Mosque into a ruin haunted by the ghost of Malcolm X. In prisons he sits in judgment of every Muslim and his martyrdom is a chicken that has come home to roost wherever Black Muslims congregate.

The third and perhaps most important reason for the decline of the Muslims in the prisons is the inexplicable failure of the outside officials of the Nation of Islam to render any legal assistance to the Muslims behind the walls. Muslim inmates, who wanted to take the California Department of Corrections into court in order to win their constitutional right to practice their religion while in prison, were forced to the ideological humiliation of asking the white devils of the American Civil Liberties Union to represent them in court.

In 1963 the Los Angeles Police Department raided Muhammad's Mosque No. 27, and in the process they shot the place up, wounding several Muslims and killing one. In the aftermath, through some strange inversion of justice, a score of Muslims were hauled up on charges ranging from disturbing the peace to assault with intent to commit murder. The incident received international publicity and became a cause in the black ghetto. It was a confrontation of the white power structure by the extremist wing of the black revolution.

As the case progressed through the courts, with legal wrangling and changes of attorneys at every step, the attention of black America was focused on the case to see how the courts would treat such an outrageous case. The Muslims lost the case, the two black bourgeois attorneys who handled the case, Earl Broady and Loren Miller, were both soon appointed to judgeships by Governor Brown—Miller to the Municipal Court and Broady to the Superior Court—and four Black Muslims were sent to prison.

After they arrived in prison, officials separated them by sending each man to a separate institution. They did this because Black Muslim inmates looked upon these men as heroes in that they were political prisoners who had fallen in the line of duty, not for committing petty crimes. Even though these men were heroes to the Nation of Islam, it became something of a scandal when the officials of the Nation outside failed to come to their heroes' aid with any legal support, so that they were reduced to the common practice of petitioning the courts *in propria persona* or appealing to the American Civil Liberties Union.

For these reasons and others less starkly dramatic, the Nation of Islam is dead in prisons, and it would take a visit by Allah in person to revive it. What black inmates now look to with rising hopes is the cry for Black Power and an elaboration of its details in the name of Malcolm X. In this connection, the most popular books being read by black inmates in prisons today, Black Muslims and just plain old fed-up Negroes, are: *The Autobiography of Malcolm X, Malcolm X Speaks, Home, Call the Keeper, The Wretched of the Earth, Negroes with Guns,* and *Che Guevara on Guerrilla Warfare*—none of which lead to Mecca.

February, 1967

PSYCHOLOGY:

THE BLACK BIBLE

This book, already recognized around the world as a classic study of the psychology of oppressed peoples, is now known among the militants of the black liberation movement in America as "the Bible."

Written by a black man who was born in Martinique and educated in Paris, who reached the apex of his genius in the crucible of the Algerian Revolution, Fanon's book is itself an historical event. For it marks a very significant moment in the history of the movement of the colonized peoples of the world—in their quest for national liberation, the modernization of their economies, and security against the never-ending intrigues of the imperialist nations.

During a certain stage in the psychological transformation of a subjected people who have begun struggling for their freedom, an impulse to violence develops in the collective unconscious. The oppressed people feel an

The Wretched of the Earth, BY FRANZ FANON. EVERGREEN PAPERBACK, $1.95. FICTION. 255 PP.

uncontrollable desire to kill their masters. But the feeling itself gives rise to myriad troubles, for the people, when they first became aware of the desire to strike out against the slavemaster, shrink from this impulse in terror. Violence then turns in upon itself and the oppressed people fight among themselves: they kill each other, and do all the things to each other which they would, in fact, like to do to the master. Intimidated by the superior armed might of the oppressor, the colonial people feel that he is invincible and that it is futile to even dream of confronting him.

When the revolutionary impulse to strike out against the oppressor is stifled, distortions in the personality appear. During the Algerian Revolution, Fanon worked in a hospital in Algeria. A psychiatrist, there he was able to observe carefully Algerians who had caved in psychologically under the pressures of a revolutionary situation. *The Wretched of the Earth* contains an appendix in which Fanon introduces several of these case histories, tracing the revolutionary impulse and attempts to evade it through the psyches of his patients.

Not all of Fanon's patients were Algerian colonial subjects. French policemen who were bothered by the brutality with which they were surrounded and in which they were involved, French soldiers who had inflicted despicable tortures on prisoners, were often confronted with situations in which their rationalizations broke down and they found themselves face to face with their own merciless deeds.

The rare significance of this book is that it contains the voice of a revolutionary black intellectual speaking directly to his own people and showing them the way to harness their forces. Fanon teaches that the key factor is to focus all the hatreds and violence on their true target—the oppressor. From then on, says Fanon, be implacable. The same point is made by Leroi Jones in his play, *Dutchman,* when his character, Clay, screams to the white woman who had tormented him, "A little murder will make us all sane again" [Speaking of black people *vis à vis* whites]. What this book does is legitimize the revolutionary impulse to violence. It teaches colonial subjects that it is perfectly normal for them to want to rise up and cut off the heads of the slavemasters, that it is a way to achieve their manhood, and that they must oppose the oppressor in order to experience themselves as men.

In the aftermath of Watts, and all the other uprisings that have set the ghettos of America ablaze, it is obvious that there is very little difference in the way oppressed people feel and react, whether they are oppressed in Algeria by the French, in Kenya by the British, in Angola by the Portuguese, or in Los Angeles by Yankee Doodle.

French philosopher Jean-Paul Sartre wrote an introduction to this book, which, he says, needed no introduction by anyone. Sartre's introduction is itself a masterpiece. Interpreting Fanon's thought for a white audience, Sartre has rendered a valuable service in driving home to the reader that this is a book he dare not pass up.

January 15, 1967

ROBERT KENNEDY'S PRISON

Mounted on the tired back of that worthy steed, the War on Poverty, the fair-haired knight of the Liberal Round Table, Senator Robert F. Kennedy, swept through San Francisco today like a storm that doesn't exist. Watching him perform before his favorite audience, the class of social workers who have developed a vested interest in the existence of poverty, I sat in the press section of the Nourse Auditorium digging this cast. This was my first time ever seeing him in person and I was conscious of the millions of words that had gone to make up his image, and I felt sick in my stomach that I had waded through so many of the words written about him.

I sat up close and got a good look at his mug. I had seen that face so many times before—hard, bitter, scurvy —all those things. I had seen his face on the bodies of night-time burglars who had been in prison for at least ten years. Robert Kennedy has been in some prison of his character for a long time. He's a convict, possibly a lifer, and I got the impression that he lives, like convicts, by one law and one law alone: I shall do only that which is expedient for survival so that I will have one more chance outside of these chains.

It has to be that; why else would a young, intelligent man sit with a sometimes serious demeanor while a battalion of lackeys paraded before the committee to submit a bunch of bullshit statistics and reports couched in a gobbledygook that even they didn't understand. Rotten Republicans and degenerate Democrats, I thought to myself. There sits our Robin Hood, the hope of the poor. And how terrible is the situation of those in America with grievances against the functioning of the system. Our Robin Hood looked too greedy to be great, too white to be all right.

"I love the poor," Kennedy seemed to be saying with his every motion, his every little petty, stock question. He wore the aura of the idol-smasher. He was the bad boy on the committee, the only one who contained the potential in his image to ask the scandalous questions. The other two members of the committee, Senator Murphy of California and Senator Clark of Pennsylvania, bore no promise except in its negative proportions. Murphy was like an old putrid watchdog, standing point before the master's mansion, bent on seeing to it that nothing got out and nothing got in. Nothing did. Except a foul odor reminiscent of the stench of the blind, complacent rich in the hour before their doom.

As I left the auditorium, I said to myself: We don't need a War on Poverty. What we need is a war on the rich.

May 10, 1967

THE COURAGE TO KILL: MEETING THE PANTHERS

While confined in California's Vacaville Prison after the Oakland shoot-out, Cleaver managed to smuggle out the following letter describing his first encounter with the Black Panthers.

I fell in love with the Black Panther Party immediately upon my first encounter with it; it was literally love at first sight. It happened one night at a meeting in a dingy little storefront on Scott Street in the Fillmore district, the heart of San Francisco's black ghetto. It was February 1967. The meeting was the latest in a series of weekly meetings held by a loose coalition functioning under the name of the Bay Area Grassroots Organizations Planning Committee. The purpose of the coalition was to coordinate three days of activities with the worthy ambition of involving the total black community in mass action commemorating the fourth anniversary of the assassination of Malcolm X. The highlight and culmination of the memorial was to be the appearance of Sister Betty Shabazz, Malcolm X's widow, who was to deliver the keynote speech at a mass meeting at the Bayview Community Center in Hunter's Point.

Among the topics on the agenda for this fortuitous meeting was the question of providing security for Sister Betty during the twenty-four hours she was to be our guest in the Bay Area. There was a paranoia around—which I did not share—that assassins by the dozens were lurking everywhere for the chance to shoot Sister Betty down. This fear, real or imagined, kept everybody uptight.

I had arrived at the meeting late, changing at the last minute a previous decision not to attend at all. I was pissed off at everyone in the room. Taking a seat with my back to the door I sat there with, I'm sure, a scornful frown of disdain upon my face. Roy Ballard (if the normal brain had three cylinders his would have one) sat opposite me, across the circle formed by the placement of the chairs. He, above all, understood the expression on my face, for he had done the most to put it there; this accounted, I thought, for the idiot grin on his own.

On Roy's left sat Ken Freeman, chairman of the now defunct Black Panther Party of Northern California, who always looked to me like Dagwood, with his huge round bifocals and the bald spot in the front of his natural. On Roy's right sat a frightened-looking little mulatto who seemed to live by the adage, "It's better to remain silent and be thought a fool than to open one's mouth and remove all doubt." He probably adopted that rule from observing his big fat yellow wife, who was seated on his right and who had said when I walked in, just loud enough for me to hear, "Shit! I thought we agreed after last week's meeting that *he* wouldn't be allowed to attend any more meetings!"

Next to her sat Jack Trueblood, a handsome, earnest youth in a black Russian cap who represented San Francisco State College's Black Students Union and who always accepted whatever tasks were piled upon him, insuring that he would leave each weekly meeting with a heavy load. On his right sat a girl named Lucky. I could never tell why they called her that—not, I'm sure, because she happened to be Roy Ballard's old lady; maybe because she had such a beautiful smile.

Between Lucky and myself sat Marvin Jackmon, who was known as a poet, because after Watts went up in flames he had composed a catchy ditty entitled "Burn, Baby, Burn!" and a play entitled *Flowers for the Trashman*. (It is hard for me to write objectively about Marvin. My association with him, dating from the third week of December 1966, ended in mutual bitterness with the closing of the Black House. After getting out of prison that month, he was the first person I hooked up with. Along with Ed Bullins, a young playwright who now has a few things going for himself off-Broadway, and Willie Dale, who had been in San Quentin with me and was trying to make it as a singer, we had founded the Black House in January 1967. Within the next two months the Black House, located in San Francisco, became the center of non-Establishment black culture throughout the Bay Area.)

On my right sat Bill Sherman, an ex-member of the Communist Party and at that time a member of the Central Committee of the Black Panther Party of

Northern California. Next to Bill was Victoria Durant, who dressed with what the black bourgeoisie would call "style" or, better yet, "class." She seemed so out of place at those meetings. We were supposed to be representing the common people—grassroots—and here was Victoria ready to write out a $50 check at the drop of a hat. She represented as everyone knew, the local clique of black Democrats who wanted inside info on everything even hinting of "organizing" in their stomping grounds—even if the price of such info was a steady flow of $50 checks.

Then there was Marianne Waddy, who kept everybody guessing because no one was ever sure of where or what she really was. One day she'd be dressed in flowing African gowns with her hair wrapped up in a pretty *skashok*, the perfect picture of the young Afro-American lady who had established a certain identity and relationship to traditional African culture. The next day she would be dressed like a man and acting like a man who would cut the first throat that got in his way.

Next to Marianne sat a sneaky-looking fellow called Nasser Shabazz. Sitting between Nasser and Ken Freeman, completing the circle, was Vincent Lynch, as smooth and black as the ebony statues he had brought back from his trip to Nigeria and the only member of the Black Panther Party of Northern California I ever liked or thought was sincere. Somewhere in the room, too, was Ann Lynch, Vincent's wife, with their bright-eyed little son, Patrice Lumumba Lynch. Ann was the head of Black Care, the women's auxiliary to this Panther Party. These sisters spent all of their time talking about the impending violent stage of the black revolution, which was inevitable, and how they, the women, must be prepared to care for the men who would be wounded in battle.

I had come out of prison with plans to revive the Organization of Afro-American Unity, the vehicle finally settled upon by Malcolm X to spearhead the black revolution. The OAAU had never really got off the ground, for it was stopped by the assassin's bullets that felled Malcolm on the stage of the Audubon Ballroom in New York City. I was amazed that no one else had moved to continue Malcolm's work in the name of the organization he had chosen, which seemed perfect to me and also logically necessary in terms of historical continuity. The three-day memorial, which was but part of the overall plan to revive the OAAU, was to be used as a forum for launching the revival. In January, I had put the plan on paper and circulated it throughout the Bay Area, then issued a general call for a meeting to establish a temporary steering committee that would see after things until the start of the memorial. At this time we would have a convention, found the Bay Area branch of the Organization of Afro-American Unity, and elect officers whom Sister Betty Shabazz would install, giving the whole effort her blessings in a keynote address on the final day of the memorial.

By February the plan had been torn to shreds. If the plan was a pearl, then I had certainly cast it before swine, and the biggest swine of all, Roy Ballard, had hijacked the plan and turned it into a circus. It soon became clear that if the OAAU was to be reborn, it would not be with the help of this crew, because all they could see was the pageantry of the memorial. Beyond that, their eyes blotted out all vision. Far from wanting to see an organization develop that would put an end to the archipelago of one-man showcase groups that plagued the black community with division, they had each made it their sacred cause to insure the survival of their own splinter group.

From the beginning, when the plan was first put before them, they took up each separate aspect and chewed it until they were sure it was either maimed for life or dead. Often after an idea had gone around the circle, if it still showed signs of life they would pounce upon it and rend it some more. When they finished, all that was left of the original plan was a pilgrimage to the site where a sixteen-year-old black youth, Matthew Johnson, had been murdered by a white cop; putting some pictures of Malcolm X on the walls of the Bayview Community Center; a hysterical speech by Ken Freeman; and twenty-four hours of Sister Betty Shabazz's time.

In all fairness, however, I must confess that the whole plan was impossible to achieve, mostly because it did not take into account certain negative aspects of the black man's psychological heritage from four hundred years of oppression here in Babylon. Then, too, I was an outsider. Having gone to prison from Los Angeles, I had been paroled to San Francisco. I was an interloper unfolding a program to organize *their* community. Fatal. It didn't matter to them that we were dealing with the concept of the Black Nation, of colonized Afro-America, and that all the boundaries separating our people were the stupid impositions of the white oppressors and had to be obliterated. Well, no matter; I had failed. Proof of my failure was Roy Ballard, sitting there before me like a gaunt buzzard, presiding over the carcass of a dream.

Suddenly the room fell silent. The crackling undercurrent that for weeks had made it impossible to get one's point across when one had the floor was gone; there was only the sound of the lock clicking as the front door opened, and then the soft shuffle of feet moving quietly toward the circle. Shadows danced on the walls. From the tension showing on the faces of the people before me, I thought the cops were invading the meeting, but there was a deep female gleam leaping out of one of the women's eyes that no cop who ever lived could elicit. I recognized that gleam out of the recesses of my soul, even though I had never seen it before in my life: the total admiration of a black woman for a black man. I spun round in my seat and saw the most beautiful sight I had ever seen: four black men wearing black berets, powder blue shirts, black leather jackets, black trousers, shiny black shoes—and each with a gun! In front was Huey P. Newton with a riot pump shotgun in his right hand, barrel pointed down to the floor. Beside him was Bobby Seale, the handle of a .45 caliber automatic showing from its holster on his right hip, just below the hem of his jacket. A few steps behind Seale was Bobby Hutton, the barrel of his shotgun at his feet. Next to him was Sherwin Forte, an M1 carbine with a banana clip cradled in his arms.

Roy Ballard jumped to his feet. Licking his lips, he said, "For those of you who've never met the brothers, these are the Oakland Panthers."

"You're wrong," said Huey P. Newton. "We're not

the Oakland Panthers. We happen to live in Oakland. Our name is the Black Panther Party."

With that the Panthers seated themselves in chairs along the wall, outside the circle. Every eye in the room was riveted upon them. What amazed me was that Roy Ballard did not utter one word in contradiction, nor was there any other yakkity-yak around the room. There was absolute silence. Even little Patrice Lumumba Lynch seemed to sit up and take notice.

Where was my mind at? Blown! Racing through time, racing through the fog of a perspective that had just been shattered into a thousand fragments. Who are these cats? I wondered at them, checking them out carefully. They were so cool and it seemed to me not unconscious of the electrifying effect they were having on everybody in the room. Then I recalled a chance remark that Marvin Jackmon had once made. We were discussing the need for security at the Black House because the crowds were getting larger and larger and we had had to bodily throw out a cat who was high and acting like he owned the place. I said that Marvin, Ed, Dale and I had better each get ourself a gun. As I elaborated on the necessity as I saw it, Marvin said: "You need to forget about the Black House and go across the bay and get with Bobby Seale." And then he laughed.

"Who is Bobby Seale?" I asked him.

At first he gave no answer, he seemed to be carefully considering what to say. Finally he said, "He's arming some brothers across the bay." Though I pressed him, he refused to go into it any further, and at the time it didn't seem important to me, so I forgot about it. Now, sitting there looking at those Panthers, I recalled the incident with Marvin. I looked at him. He seemed to have retreated inside himself, sitting there looking like a skinny black Buddha with something distasteful and menacing on his mind.

"Do you brothers want to make a speech at the memorial?" Roy Ballard asked the Panthers.

"Yes," Bobby Seale said.

"O.K.," said Ballard. "We have the program broken down into subjects: Politics, Economics, Self-Defense and Black Culture. Now which section do you brothers want to speak under?" This was the sort of question which in my experience had always signaled the beginning of a two-hour debate with this group.

"It doesn't matter what section we speak under," Huey said. "Our message is one and the same. We're going to talk about black people arming themselves in a political fashion to exert organized force in the political arena to see to it that their desires and needs are met. Otherwise there will be a political consequence. And the only culture worth talking about is a revolutionary culture. So it doesn't matter what heading you put on it, we're going to talk about political power growing out of the barrel of a gun."

"O.K.," Roy Ballard said. He paused, then added, "Let's put it under Politics." Then he went on to start the specific discussion of security for Sister Betty, who would pick her up at the airport, etc. Bobby Seale was jotting down notes in a little black book. The other Panthers sat quietly, watchfully.

Three days before the start of the memorial, I received a phone call from Los Angeles. The man on the other end identified himself as Hakim Jamal, Malcolm X's cousin by marriage. He would be arriving with Sister Betty, he said, and both of them wanted to talk with me. They had liked, it turned out, an article on Malcolm that I had written and that was published in *Ramparts*. We agreed that when they got in from the airport I would meet them at the *Ramparts* office in San Francisco.

On the day that Sister Betty and Hakim Jamal were to arrive in San Francisco, I was sitting in my office tinkering with some notes for an article. One of the secretaries burst through the door. Her face was white with fear and she was shouting, "We're being invaded! We're being invaded!"

I couldn't tell just who her invaders were. Were the Chinese coming? Had the CIA finally decided to do *Ramparts* in? Then she said, "There are about twenty men outside with guns!"

I knew that Hakim Jamal and Sister Betty had arrived with their escort of armed Black Panthers.

"Don't worry," I said, "they're friends."

"Friends?" she gasped. I left her there with her eyes bugging out of her head and rushed to the front of the building.

I waded through *Ramparts* staff jammed into the narrow hallway, fending off the frightened inquiries by repeating, "It's all right, it's all right." The lobby resembled certain photographs coming out of Cuba the day Castro took Havana. There were guns everywhere, pointed toward the ceiling like metallic blades of grass growing up out of the sea of black faces beneath the black berets of the Panthers. I found Hakim Jamal and Sister Betty surrounded by a knot of Panthers, who looked calm and self-possessed in sharp contrast to the chaotic reactions their appearance had set off. Outside where Broadway ran in four lanes to feed the freeway on-ramp and to receive the heavy traffic from the off-ramp, a massive traffic jam was developing and sirens could be heard screaming in the distance as cops sped our way.

I took Jamal and Sister Betty to an office down the hall. We talked for about fifteen minutes about Malcolm. Sister Betty, her eyes concealed behind dark glasses, said nothing after we were introduced. She looked cool enough on the surface, but it was clear that she felt hard-pressed. Huey P. Newton was standing at the window, shotgun in hand, looking down into the upturned faces of a horde of police. I left the room to get Sister Betty a glass of water, squeezing past Bobby Seale and what seemed like a battalion of Panthers in the hall guarding the door. Seale's face was a chiseled mask of determination.

A few yards down the hall, Warren Hinckle III, editor of *Ramparts,* was talking to a police lieutenant.

"What's the trouble?" the lieutenant asked, pointing at the Black Panthers with their guns.

"No trouble," Hinckle said. "Everything is under control."

The policeman seemed infuriated by this answer. He stared at Bobby Seale for a moment and then stalked outside. While I was in the lobby a TV cameraman, camera on his shoulder, forced his way through the front door and started taking pictures. Two white boys who worked at *Ramparts* stopped the TV man and informed him that he was trespassing on private property. When he refused to leave they picked him up and threw him out the door, camera and all.

When it was agreed that it was time to leave, Huey

Newton took control. Mincing no words, he sent five of his men out first to clear a path through the throng of spectators clustered outside the door, most of whom were cops. He dispatched a phalanx of ten Panthers fast on their heels, with Hakim Jamal and Sister Betty concealed in their midst. Newton himself, along with Bobby Seale and three other Panthers, brought up the rear.

I went outside and stood on the steps of *Ramparts* to observe the departure. When Huey left the building, the TV cameraman who had been tossed out was grinding away with his camera. Huey took an envelope from his pocket and held it up in front of the camera, blocking the lens.

"Get out of the way!" the TV man shouted. When Huey continued to hold the envelope in front of the lens, the TV man started cursing, and reached out and knocked Huey's hand away with his fist. Huey coolly turned to one of the score of cops watching and said:

"Officer, I want you to arrest this man for assault."

An incredulous look came into the cop's face, then he blurted out: "If I arrest anybody it'll be you!"

Huey turned on the cameraman, again placing the envelope in front of the lens. Again the cameraman reached out and knocked Huey's hand away. Huey reached out, snatched the cameraman by the collar and slammed him up against the wall, sending him spinning and staggering down the sidewalk, trying to catch his breath and balance the camera on his shoulder at the same time.

Bobby Seale tugged at Huey's shirt sleeve. "C'mon, Huey, let's get out of here."

Huey and Bobby started up the sidewalk toward their

car. The cops stood there on the point, poised as though ready to start shooting at a given signal.

"Don't turn your backs on these back-shooting dogs!" Huey called out to Bobby and the other three Panthers. By this time the other Panthers with Sister Betty and Jamal had gotten into cars and melted into the traffic jam. Only these five were still at the scene.

At that moment a big, beefy cop stepped forward. He undid the little strap holding his pistol in his holster and started shouting at Huey, "Don't point that gun at me! Stop pointing that gun at me!" He kept making gestures as though he was going for his gun.

This was the most tense of moments. Huey stopped in his tracks and stared at the cop.

"Let's split, Huey! Let's split!" Bobby Seale was saying.

Ignoring him, Huey walked to within a few feet of the cop and said, "What's the matter, you got an itchy finger?"

The cop made no reply.

"You want to draw your gun?" Huey asked him.

The other cops were calling out for this cop to cool it, to take it easy, but he didn't seem to be able to hear them. He was staring into Huey's eyes, measuring him.

"O.K.," Huey said. "You big fat racist pig, draw your gun!"

The cop made no move.

"Draw it, you cowardly dog!" Huey pumped a round into the chamber of the shotgun. "I'm waiting," he said, and stood there waiting for the cop to draw.

All the other cops moved back out of the line of fire. I moved back, too, onto the top step of *Ramparts*. I was thinking, staring at Huey surrounded by all those cops and daring one of them to draw, "Goddam, that nigger is c-r-a-z-y!"

Then the cop facing Huey gave it up. He heaved a heavy sigh and lowered his head. Huey literally laughed in his face and then went off up the street at a jaunty pace, disappearing in a blaze of dazzling sunlight.

"Work out, soul brother!" I was shouting to myself. "You're the baddest motherfucker I've ever seen!" I went back into *Ramparts* and we all stood around chattering excitedly, discussing what we had witnessed with disbelief.

"*Who was that?*" asked Vampira, Warren Hinckle's little sister.

"That was Huey P. Newton," I said, "Minister of Defense of the Black Panther Party."

"Boy, is he gutsy!" she said dreamily.

"Yeah," I agreed. "He's out of sight!"

The quality in Huey P. Newton's character that I had seen that morning in front of *Ramparts* and that I was to see demonstrated over and over again after I joined the Black Panther Party was *courage*. I had called it "crazy," as people often do to explain away things they do not understand. I don't mean the courage "to stand up and be counted," or even the courage it takes to face certain death. I speak of that revolutionary courage it takes to pick up a gun with which to oppose the oppressor of one's people. That's a different kind of courage.

Oppressed people, Fanon points out, kill each other all the time. A glance through any black newspaper will prove that black people in America kill each other with regularity. This is the internalized violence of oppressed people. Angered by the misery of their lives but cowed by the overt superior might of the oppressor, the oppressed people shrink from striking out at the true objects of their hostility and strike instead at their more defenseless brothers and sisters near at hand. Somehow this seems safer, less fraught with dire consequences, as though one is less dead when shot down by one's brother than when shot down by the oppressor. It is merely criminal to take up arms against one's brother, but to step outside the vicious circle of the internalized violence of the oppressed and take up arms against the oppressor is to step outside of life itself, to step outside of the structure of this world, to enter, almost alone, the no-man's-land of revolution.

Huey P. Newton took that step. For the motto of the Black Panther Party he chose a quotation from Mao Tse-tung's *Little Red Book*: "We are advocates of the abolition of war; we do not want war; but war can only be abolished through war; and in order to get rid of the gun it is necessary to pick up the gun."

When I decided to join the Black Panther Party the only hang-up I had was with its name. I was still clinging to my conviction that we owed it to Malcolm to pick up where he left off. To me, this meant building the organization that he had started. Picking up where Malcolm left off, however, had different meanings for different people. For cats like Marvin Jackmon, for instance, it meant returning to the ranks of Elijah Muhammad's Nation of Islam, denouncing Malcolm as a heretic and pledging loyalty to Elijah, all in Malcolm's name. For Huey, it meant implementing the program that Malcolm advocated. When that became clear to me, I knew what Huey P. Newton was all about.

For the revolutionary black youth of today, time

starts moving with the coming of Malcolm X. Before Malcolm, time stands still, going down in frozen steps into the depths of the stagnation of slavery. Malcolm talked shit, and talking shit is the iron in a young nigger's blood. Malcolm mastered language and used it as a sword to slash his way through the veil of lies that for four hundred years gave the white man the power of the word. Through the breach in the veil, Malcolm saw all the way to national liberation, and he showed us the rainbow and the golden pot at its end. Inside the golden pot, Malcolm told us, was the tool of liberation. Huey P. Newton, one of the millions of black people who listened to Malcolm, lifted the golden lid off the pot and blindly, trusting Malcolm, stuck his hand inside and grasped the tool. When he withdrew his hand and looked to see what he held, he saw the gun, cold in its metal and implacable in its message: Death-Life, Liberty or Death, mastered by a black hand at last! Huey P. Newton is the ideological descendant, heir and successor of Malcolm X. Malcolm prophesied the coming of the gun to the black liberation struggle. Huey P. Newton picked up the gun and pulled the trigger, freeing the genie of black revolutionary violence in Babylon.

The genie of black revolutionary violence is here, and it says that the oppressor has no rights which the oppressed are bound to respect. The genie also has a question for white Americans: which side do you choose? Do you side with the oppressor or with the oppressed? The time for decision is upon you. The cities of America have tested the first flames of revolution. But a hotter fire rages in the hearts of black people today: total liberty for black people or total destruction for America.

The prospects, I confess, do not look promising. Besides being a dumb nation, America is mad with white racism. Whom the gods would destroy, they first make mad. Perhaps America has been mad far too long to make any talk of sanity relevant now. But there is a choice and it will be made, by decision or indecision, by action or inaction, by commission or omission. Black people have made their choice; a revolutionary generation that has the temerity to say to America that Huey P. Newton must be set free, also invested with the courage to kill, pins its hopes on the revolutionary's faith and says, with Che: "Wherever death may surprise us, it will be welcome, provided that this, our battlecry, reach some receptive ear, that another hand reach out to pick up weapons, and that other fighting men come forward to intone our funeral dirge with the staccato of machine guns and new cries of battle and victory."

June 15, 1968

INTRODUCTION TO
THE BIOGRAPHY OF
HUEY P. NEWTON

I remember once during the trial of Huey P. Newton, a lawyer stopped me in the hall of the Alameda County Courthouse. He was very nervous, and he said, "They are crucifying Huey in there—they are turning him into another Jesus." And I remember almost instinctively replying, "Yes, Huey is our Jesus, but we want him down from the cross."

The tendency to look upon Huey as being above and beyond others, to view Huey as being different from everybody else, I think this is something that happens; I know that it happens to members of the Black Panthers, and it happens more and more to black people who have an understanding about Huey, and who know a little about his leadership of the party and some of the very courageous stands that he has taken. When you think of Huey, along with his followers, out on the streets of Oakland at night, in alleys, on dark streets, confronted by racist pig cops who are known to be very brutal, very vicious and murderous in their approach to black people, you cannot help but be amazed and fascinated by his seriousness, by his willingness and readiness to lay down his life in defense of the rights of his people, and his own rights, his human rights and his Constitutional rights.

I cannot help but say that Huey P. Newton is the baddest motherfucker ever to set foot inside of history. Huey has a very special meaning to black people, because for four hundred years black people have been wanting to do exactly what Huey Newton did, that is, to stand up in front of the most deadly tentacle of the white racist power structure, and to defy that deadly tentacle, and to tell that tentacle that he will not accept the aggression and the brutality, and that if he is moved against, he will retaliate in kind. Huey Newton is a classical revolutionary figure. His imagination is constantly at work, conjuring up strategies and tactics that apply classical revolutionary principles to the situations confronting black people here in America.

Much has been written about Huey P. Newton, Minister of Defense of the Black Panther Party, but most of what has been written, it seems to me, obscures his essential character, as it fails really to show Huey in motion. The man who knows Huey perhaps better than anyone else is Bobby Seale, Chairman of the Black Panther Party, who, along with Huey, organized the party. Bobby has known Huey Newton for approximately eight years, dating back to their days at Merritt College in Oakland. He has had a chance to observe Huey under varying circumstances and in various situations, and he has the kind of appreciation and understanding of Huey that come only from careful observation, that become a fixation on what makes this man, Huey Newton, tick.

Because Bobby united with Huey and, in a very real sense, placed his life in Huey's hands, he had very good reason for checking out Huey very closely, and he arrived at the conclusion that it was a proper and safe thing to do. I would say that, knowing Bobby and Huey, and knowing the relationship that exists between the two of them, Bobby had no choice, and felt compelled to place his life in Huey's hands. You could almost say that his admiration and respect for Huey is a sort of worship, and I don't mean this in any religious sense, but in the sense of Newton as a man who is motivated by a deep and burning preoccupation and concern with the plight of black people, who is seeking solutions to the problems of black people, and who recognizes that it is going to take a very fundamental action on a revolutionary level to cut into the oppression and to motivate people, black people, to take a revolutionary stance against the decadent racist system that is oppressing them.

Bob Scheer and I took Bobby Seale down to Carmel, California, and we secluded ourselves in a little cabin, and placed a tape recorder in front of Bobby, and put a microphone in his hands, and asked him to talk about Huey P. Newton. Having myself joined the Black Panther Party, and accepted Huey P. Newton as my leader, I find myself sharing with Bobby Seale the same attitude toward Huey—the same willingness to place my life in his hands, the same confidence that Huey will do the right thing at any given moment, that his instincts are sound, and that there is nothing to do but follow Huey and back him up.

October 26, 1968

MY FATHER AND
STOKELY CARMICHAEL

My father, at whose house I had spent the night after arriving in Chicago, accompanied me to the SNCC office. "Jesus," he said, "this is really rock bottom. This is the poorest section of the Negro part of town. Why would anyone want to set up an office down here?" My father is not too hep to the action these days. He's like many old Negroes: they woke up on the white man late in their lives and are very bitter to learn that they have been tricked.

The building was an old wooden apartment house about five stories high with a faded brownstone exterior. You had second thoughts about opening the door to go in. SNCC was on the third floor. We made our way up the dark stairs and knocked on the door.

"Who is it?" A girl's voice filtered through the door. It must have been only a ritual you go through before opening your door to anyone, because when I answered "Eldridge" the door was opened. She'd never seen me, but she stepped back to let us come in. Inside, a record player was booming out John Coltrane. A chubby little baby was romping about on the floor, and an intense young black man was hunched over a typewriter painfully pecking at the keys. I explained who I was, and said I had arranged to meet Stokely Carmichael.

The girl regarded me narrowly for a moment, her intelligent brown eyes emitting a very soft twinkle. Softness was her central quality. She looked soft and warm, soft and brown, and her hair was worn in the natural style of blacks who are no longer ashamed of the hair with which their race is endowed. We took off our coats and the girl got on the phone and started calling people to find out where Stokely was. "I know he's supposed to be here at twelve thirty," she said.

The youth at the typewriter turned out to be the son of Sarah Wright, the noted black poet. He was busy working on an essay attacking American imperialism both abroad and in the black ghettos. He kept picking up books from his desk and asking me if I had read them: *Das Kapital*, Nkrumah's *Neo-Colonialism*, *The Wretched of the Earth*.

"I want to go to Africa to study," he kept saying. "I got to get ready. I got to get my stuff together."

The girl hung up the phone and turned to me. "Stokely will be available about one o'clock."

I didn't want to hang around that office with my father until one o'clock, mainly because he had begun asking a barrage of questions: Who's Nkrumah? Who wrote that book? So I told them that I would go pick up my luggage and hustle right back. Pa and I had lunch together. Then he ran and got his camera and started snapping pictures of me. I explained to him that this was a very important assignment for me and I had better go back alone because these people might not like it if I brought anyone else along.

When I got back to the SNCC office there was another cat there. He turned out to be David Llorens, a black writer whose works I knew. He had been sent over to take me to Stokely.

We sped through the icy Chicago streets toward the house where we were to meet Carmichael. He was sitting on the couch with a telephone in his hand. In the days to come I was to be with Carmichael almost constantly and, when he was not moving, making speeches, or eating, he was on the telephone. He simply could not sit down for ten minutes without being called to the phone or feeling the urge to call someone up himself.

We ate, ran red lights to get downtown as fast as possible. Stokely was an hour late for a TV taping with Irv Kupcinet, Chicago's leading TV personality. A white lady got on the up elevator. She was reading a sheaf of papers and didn't notice us until the elevator doors closed. Then she looked to her left and flinched when she saw Cleveland Sellers, immediately averting her eyes. Then she looked to her right and there was Carmichael in his ubiquitous dark glasses. Finally, she looked back over her shoulder into my face. She suddenly grew very rigid and seemed to shrivel up. When she reached her floor she rushed from the elevator as though from some evil presence. After the doors had closed we all had a big laugh. "They can't do with us and they can't do without us," Carmichael said.

When the elevator reached Kupcinet's studio, a throng, Kupcinet in the center, was waiting. Carmichael was rushed to his seat. Center stage was set up with a coffee table surrounded on three sides by comfortable couches facing the TV cameras. Seated on one of the couches was Congressman Roman Pucinski, a member of Adam Clayton Powell's House Education and Labor Committee and a leader in the fight to strip Powell of his chairmanship. Also present were Archibald Carey, a Negro judge and the preacher of a large Negro Christian church; Rich C. Kriegel, a representative of the U.S. State Department; and Studs Terkel, a liberal Chicago radio commentator.

The show started out amiably enough with a few mild questions about Adam Clayton Powell and the then fresh news of the action against him in Congress. Congressman Pucinski rambled off all the cliches against Powell, and endorsed every one of them. Then Carmichael got to talk. He wanted to know why Pucinski and his fellow congressmen were so willing to strip Powell of his position but wouldn't raise a finger to oust congressmen from Mississippi and Alabama who held their seats because Negroes had been intimidated, murdered, and kept from voting.

Carmichael then talked about Vietnam. He had brought with him a briefcase filled with authoritative material because he wanted to be able to back up every remark with quotes from respectable types. Congressman Pucinski, the man from State, and Judge Carey carried the ball for the Johnson administration, while Carmichael and Terkel emerged united against them. "I'm not being political!" Carmichael would scream. "We're discussing the lives of human beings. Men, women, and children are being butchered in Vietnam every day. I'm talking about murder. MURDER! DO YOU HEAR? I'm talking about the fact that if I kill a man with slanted eyes on the street I go to jail, but if I do it in Vietnam I get a medal. I'm talking about who has the right to tell me to go commit murder. Who has the right to define for me who my enemies are? Killing another person is the most serious step that a man can take. If I ever reach the point where I want to kill someone, I'm going to be the one who makes that decision."

Pucinski, Carey, and Kriegel couldn't understand why Carmichael said that he would not fight in that war, or why Terkel was so concerned about America becoming a nation of moral monsters. After it became clear that it was hopeless to try to communicate on those issues, Carmichael said, "Hey, Bobby Dylan has the perfect line for you cats: 'You know something is happening but you don't know what it is, do you, Mr. Jones.'" Just before the show broke up, Carey sighed heavily, admitted that he was confused and that most of what had been said that day had gone over his head. The State Department's man made an announcement that he was opening a recruiting office in the area and he gave a long list of the various skills in which he was interested. When he had finished, David Llorens said, "He didn't say poets; he doesn't want any poets!" It was our luck to get into the same elevator with the man from the State Department. All the way down David Llorens kept asking him, "Why didn't you ask for poets?" And the State Department man kept answering, "I didn't read all the list, I didn't read all the list."

As we drove away from the studio, the radio was blowing black music. It was during this drive that I began to form my picture of Carmichael. The record

"Tell It Like It Is" began playing. This is a soulful song, the blues, of the people. When it first came on, Carmichael gave a loud whoop, clapped his hands and began singing along with the radio. I wondered how Martin Luther King or Whitney Young or Roy Wilkins would have reacted to the same music.

We headed down to the ghetto to talk to the black nationalists at the headquarters of a group called ACT for Freedom. There were about two hundred black radicals inside waiting for Stokely. The first question took us all by surprise. "Stokely," a cat with a Jomo Kenyatta skull cap asked, "What're you doing downtown talking to white folks? Why don't you have time for your own people?"

"I don't know what you mean when you say that I don't have any time for my own people. For the past six years my entire life has gone to my people."

"Then why is it that every time you come to Chicago," another cat asked, "you always come to talk to white folks?"

This was followed by a barrage of similar statements. They knew Stokely was going to speak that evening at the University of Chicago. At least ten people voiced similar points of view, and they became increasingly bitter. I was surprised to see that Stokely was sitting in front of the throng with his legs crossed, listening very calmly to criticism that had become very personal. He broke his silence at one point to say, "My record speaks for itself," but mostly he just heard them out. One of them quoted LeRoi Jones on the futility of talking to white folks. Then they quieted down to hear Stokely defend himself.

"I came to Chicago to speak at the University because

some people there got together, set up a meeting, sold
tickets, and asked me to come. That was a paid engage-
ment. We need money to operate, brothers and sisters.
Those are the hard facts of life. You cats sit here and
talk all this shit, but what are you doing? If you want
me to come here and speak to you, why don't you organize a meeting and then ask me to come? Are you
willing to finance my activity? Are you? This is one of
the major pitfalls of black people. We want to control
our organizations, but we are not willing to support
them. Then when we see someone else trying to do the
job the best he can, instead of lending a hand, we lay
back and take pot shots at him.

"I'm going to tell you cats just like it is. My base is
in the South. I have support in the South. But you cats
are not really with me. The police could grab me and
beat my head in, and you cats won't do a goddam thing
about it. But when the police messed with me in Atlanta, niggers got together and tore the town up—and
they let me go. The police let me go, because they
knew that the black people weren't going to just stand
around and let them fuck over me. We've got to understand that. We've got to make the white man understand that there are 20 million black people in this
country and that when they mess with one black man
they got to mess with 20 million black people. That's
why I'm supporting Adam Clayton Powell. I'm not supporting Powell because I think he is such a shining
example to black people. I'm supporting Powell because he's the most powerful black politician this country has ever had. So when they stripped him of his
power, they were castrating a black man who was in a
position to help us.

"We have just started our drive to organize black people in the Northern ghettos. We have to proceed the best way we know how. And you cats shouldn't be waiting around for us to come in. Get up and start organizing the people. *Organize!* That is the only thing that counts."

"Stokely," one man asked, "why don't you move to Chicago and help us get rid of Martin Luther King?"

Stokely broke into a smile. The mood of the meeting had shifted, and from that moment on there was no more criticism of Stokely. It became clear that the earlier criticism was something of a ritual. The full love which they all felt for him began to flow through the room, and you could feel it in the air. "We can't be everywhere at once," Stokely answered. "And we don't want to get into a fight with King. We have enough on our hands fighting the Man. Daley would like nothing better than for SNCC to get into a fight with King. That way he could get rid of us both. If you want to get rid of King—or anybody else—it's up to you to get together right here in Chicago. There are enough black people in Chicago to take over—if you get together and get rid of the Uncle Toms. Once you start organizing you'll find that things start happening and you will be able to do anything. And don't worry about ideology. I always say that my work is my ideology. You will find that after you get going, your ideology will develop out of your struggle."

At that point, Cleveland Sellers, program coordinator for SNCC, stepped in. "I'm sorry folks, but he has to go. We're already late. We were supposed to be at the University at eight o'clock."

"Let the white folks wait!" somebody shouted from

the back of the room. "We waited four hundred years for them, so let the bastards wait on us now."

From backstage at the University hall, we could see that the ACT cats had done a very peculiar thing. They had stationed themselves around the hall at strategic points, similar to the way in which the Fruit of Islam elite guards stand at Black Muslim meetings. They were guarding Stokely. They appeared to be unarmed.

During the question period following Stokely's enthusiastically received speech, a white girl asked him who the guys standing guard were, and if he thought he needed protection from the white students.

"Do you want me to introduce you to them?" Stokely asked her. "They are a beautiful bunch of black brothers. They're looking out for me."

There has always been the drama in the black psyche in America that a generation of men would arise and go back to the South to strike the chains from the slavemasters' minds. Stokely Carmichael belongs to the first generation of Negroes who had the courage to return. The generation of Negroes who kicked off the sit-ins among black college students is different from anything that has gone before. Now it is six years later and these youngsters have grown into tough, battle-tested veterans. They have become conscious revolutionaries. Having started out trying to change the world by forcing America to re-examine its conscience, these revolutionaries have been frustrated in that approach, and they now look with scorn upon doctrines that ask them to love their enemy. Carmichael says: "I'm not in the Movement out of love. I'm in the Movement because

I hate. I hate racism and I'm out to smash it or it's going to smash me. When we first went down South, the papers tried to make it look like we wanted to sit next to Bull Connor and Ross Barnett and eat hot dogs. That's a lie. We went South to render those crackers impotent over our lives."

They went South. In this fact is contained a revolution. There is a vast difference between Negroes who are willing to go South and all those generations whose ambition was to flee the South. A cycle has been completed. The real work for the liberation of black people in America has begun.

A new cycle has begun in another way, too: the great popular black nationalist leaders like Marcus Garvey, Elijah Muhammad, and Malcolm X all never finished high school. Stokely Carmichael is the first of his stature to receive a college degree.

The history of the national liberation struggles in Africa and in the world in general hints that the success of the struggle for liberation awaits the arrival of intellectuals who have thrown off the shackles of the slave and are willing to put their talents and genius selflessly to work for the masses. Up until now, one of the traditional complaints of the black masses has been of the treachery of black intellectuals. Most of the first rate black writers America has produced have been men with little or no formal education, such as Richard Wright and James Baldwin. And of the first rate black writers, like W. E. B. Dubois and Ralph Ellison, who have had a formal education, none until now has been able to communicate with the black masses of his time. But today the college-educated LeRoi Jones is part of a new generation of radical black writers, just as Stokely

Carmichael is part of a new generation of radical black leaders.

Among Stokely's important future plans is a trip to Africa. This trip will be a key move in SNCC's drive to internationalize black America's struggle for human rights. But contrary to a lot of doctrinaire black nationalists, Stokely believes that the most important area outside the USA, as far as forging working alliances is concerned, is Latin America. Within the next ten years, the struggle for liberation from American domination throughout Latin America will provide black America with some very important and strong allies. By turning such a hopeful eye toward Latin America, Carmichael gives a hint of a quality that is forever breaking through and which distinguishes him from a lot of black nationalists who have been overly influenced by the racist philosophy of the Black Muslims. "We've got to learn who to coalition with and who not to coalition with. We've got to make specific alliances on specific issues. My enemy's enemy is my friend. I may not love him; I may even hate him. But if he can help me get the hooks and claws of the eagle out of my throat I want to talk to him."

The Student Nonviolent Coordinating Committee has already formed an official, public alliance with the independence movement in Puerto Rico. SNCC has agreed to throw its influence behind Puerto Rican nationalists in their struggle for U.N. membership and recognition as a sovereign nation. In turn, the Puerto Rican nationalists have committed themselves to an all-out effort to raise the problem of black America before the U.N. and to lobby unceasingly for support in this effort from the Afro-Asian bloc.

Carmichael is very bitter against people who refuse to take a principled stand on the issue. He says, "When Muhammad Ali took a stand against the war in Vietnam, I was very happy, because now I had someone else to back me up. But then white America screamed on the cat and he folded up. That did not make me too happy."

The essence of what Carmichael is doing is calling for a showdown with racism. He says, "The civil rights movement was good because it demanded that blacks be admitted into the system. Now we must move beyond the stage of demanding entry, to the new stage of changing the system itself." He is calling for a showdown. In this context, he, along with all the other activists I talked with during the tour, was very resentful of the passive role the Black Muslims have been playing. "They talk strong, but they won't do anything but kill another black man," one man told me.

Each time he gave a talk, Stokely would cite *Alice in Wonderland*. "When I use a word," Humpty Dumpty said in rather a scornful tone, "it means just what I choose it to mean, neither more nor less."

"The question is," said Alice, "whether you *can* make words mean so many different things."

"The question is," said Humpty Dumpty, "who is to be master, that's all."

Stokely told his audiences that one of the most important aspects of the struggle for Black Power was the right to define. Black people have been the victims of white America's definitions. White people defined black people as inferior, as Negroes and niggers, as second-class citizens. By reacting to white America's definitions, the blacks allowed themselves to be put in a bag which white America controlled. But now black people must demand the right to define themselves. White America has defined black as evil, Carmichael explains. "I have a little syllogism for that. According to America, everything black is evil; I'm black; therefore I'm evil.

"There is something wrong with that," he goes on to explain, "because I'm black and I'm good." He never fails to score heavily with his audience when he says that.

His favorite example of this always elicited a hysterical response, from both black and white audiences. "Here is a perfect example of the power to define in action. During the civil rights movement, black leaders would say: 'We want to integrate.' And then white people would come along and define what integration means. They'd say: 'You want to integrate? That means that you want to marry my daughter.' What the Negro leaders had actually meant was that they wanted more jobs, better schools, housing, and an end to police brutality, and things like that. But when the whites defined integration as meaning that blacks wanted to marry their daughters, these leaders lost out by reacting to the white definition. So they ended up explaining: 'No, we don't want to marry your daughter. We don't want to be your brother-in-law, we want to be your brother. We don't want to live in your bedroom, we just want to live next door.'

"The point is that when these Negroes started reacting to these white definitions, they were backed against the wall before they knew what was happening. They had come in with an indictment that put white America on the defensive. But by allowing white America to define what integration meant, these Negroes allowed themselves and the people for whom they spoke to be placed on the defensive. That is a bunch of crap. What we must do is define our own terms. When whites come to me with that crap, I just tell them, look, 'Your daughter, your wife, your sister, your mama—the white woman is not the queen of the earth, she's not the Virgin Mary. The white woman can be made just like any other woman. Now let's move on.' We must not react to white definitions.

"When I say Black Power, I know exactly what I'm talking about. But the white man runs up to me and says, 'Black Power: that means violence, doesn't it?' I refuse to react to that. I know what I'm talking about. If the white man doesn't know what I'm talking about, that's his problem, because black people understand me and that is who I'm talking to anyway."

On this same point, Carmichael points out how forces hostile to the black liberation struggle can steal the fire of the movement by co-opting its slogans. He says that LBJ killed the civil rights movement the moment he stood before nationwide TV and said, "We shall overcome." "But he will never," Carmichael says, "stand before the nation and say, 'We want Black Power.'"

April, 1967

THE LAND
QUESTION AND
BLACK LIBERATION

The first thing that has to be realized is that it is a reality when people say that there's a "black colony" and a "white mother country." Only if this distinction is borne clearly in mind is it possible to understand that there are two different sets of political dynamics now functioning in America.

From the very beginning, Afro-America has had a land hang-up. The slaves were kidnapped on their own soil, transported thousands of miles across the ocean and set down in a strange land. They found themselves in a totally hostile situation and America became a land from which black people wanted only to flee, to escape such evil soil and those vicious creatures who had usurped it.

During slavery itself, black people learned to hate the land. From sunup to sundown, the slaves worked the land: plowing, sowing and reaping crops for somebody else, for profit they themselves would never see or taste. This is why, even today, one of the most provocative insults that can be tossed at a black is to call him a farm boy, to infer that he is from a rural area or in any way attached to an agrarian situation. In terms of seeking status in America, blacks—principally the black bourgeoisie—have come to measure their own value according to the number of degrees they are away from the soil.

Considered subhuman by the founders of America, black people have always been viewed by white Americans as un-American, as not really belonging here. As Abraham Lincoln put it, black people and white people can never live together as equals.* Therefore it would be better for the two races to separate, and since America is a rich country, naturally the whites will keep it and the inferior blacks will go somewhere else, preferably back to the darkness of African jungles where good Christian white folks found them in the first place. The snotty-nosed tag line for the freckle-faced young racists of America is to shout at a black person, "Hey, why don't you go back to Africa?"

Thus, it is not surprising that the average black man in America is schizoid on the question of his relationship to the nation as a whole, and there is a side of him that feels only the vaguest, most halting, tentative and even fleeting kinship with America. The feeling of alienation and dissociation is real and black people long ago would have readily identified themselves with another sovereignty had a viable one existed. Integra-

* "I will say, then, that I am not, nor ever have been, in favor of bringing about in any way the social and political equality of the white and black races [applause]: that I am not, nor ever have been, in favor of making voters or jurors of Negroes, nor of qualifying them to hold office, nor to intermarry with white people. . . .

"And inasmuch as they cannot so live, while they do remain together there must be the position of superior and inferior, and I as much as any other man am in favor of having the superior position assigned to the white race." Abraham Lincoln, quoted in Richard Hofstadter, *The American Political Tradition* (New York, Vintage Books, 1955).

tion was the solution to the land question offered by the mother country—i.e., by the white liberals, white radicals and black bourgeoisie, working hand in glove with the imperialists. The problem would be solved, they said, when blacks were allowed to share the land. Blacks must be allowed to feel at home in America.

This is not to imply that white liberals, radicals and the black bourgeoisie were actively involved in a conscious conspiracy with the imperialists. Rather, we speak here of a coalescence of interests and goals. Particularly in the case of white radicals, the last thing they would want to do is to help the imperialists remain in power. But a situation developed in which it became too dangerous to the overall selfish interests of the imperialists to allow the remnants of segregation to continue, thereby radicalizing black people, by forcing them to unite in order to defend their human rights.

The domestic conflict over segregation was creating for the imperialists problems on the international plane. As long as the conflict remained purely domestic, the imperialists never moved to solve the problem. But things finally reached the point where the nature of American imperialism was continually being exposed around the world because of the way black people were being treated here at "home." America's enemies missed no opportunity to point out the sham of U.S. foreign policy—the exportation of "democracy"—as evidenced by the fact that the U.S. had no democracy at home to export.

This became a very pressing problem for U.S. imperialism in its dealings with the black African governments that were cascading onto the international scene. In the so-called battle between the imperialist countries and the socialist countries for the minds of the people of the Third World, the Soviet Union and the entire world's left press continually embarrassed U.S. imperialism over the way black people were being treated. Therefore, when the federal government "joined" the civil rights movement, the imperialists in control of the government actually strengthened their own position and increased their power. Internationally, U.S. imperialism improved its image, making the con game it plays on the world, its pose as the champion of human freedom, easier. When President Johnson, the arch-hypocritic warmonger of the twentieth century, stood before the nation and shouted "We shall overcome," white liberals, radicals and the black bourgeoisie experienced a collective orgasm.

(It is interesting to note that from the very moment LBJ slobbered on the slogan "We shall overcome," thus both defiling and redefining it, the slogan was discarded by all self-respecting people in the black liberation struggle and only Martin Luther King has since had the temerity to utter it in public.)

What Johnson wanted was peace and quiet at home and an integrated army to defend "democracy" abroad. Given the international situation and the rising militancy of black people in America, the ideological tenet of integration was the perfect tool for resolving a most blatant contradiction between what U.S. imperialism practiced at home and preached abroad. To sit back and allow black people to become totally alienated from "the American dream" would create problems of major proportions for U.S. imperialism at home and abroad. It was for this reason that U.S. imperialism became a champion of integration.

White radicals, liberals and the black bourgeoisie acted from completely different motivations, but the logic of the situation threw them into a coalition with the Imperialists, and the game that was run on them was so successful that they became some of the most ardent workers for LBJ in the election of 1964. Their motivation was to implement the American dream and the conception of America as a huge melting pot. All that remained to be done, in their view, was to integrate the black ingredient into the American stew and thus usher in the millennium of black–white solidarity wherein the white working class of the mother country would join hands with the black workers from the colony and together they would march forward to the Garden of Eden.

March forward they did, not to Eden but to Detroit and armed urban guerrilla warfare. The basic flaw in the analysis and outlook of the white liberals, radicals and the black bourgeoisie is that the concept of the American melting pot completely ignores the distinction and the contradiction between the white mother country and the black colony. And the solution of Integration, based on this false outlook, was doomed from the beginning to yield only a deceptive and disillusioning result. Black people are a stolen people held in a colonial status on stolen land, and any analysis which does not acknowledge the colonial status of black people cannot hope to deal with the real problem.

As an ideological tenet, integration embodies the dream of the mother country which sees America as a huge melting pot. It seeks to pull the black colonial subjects into America and citizenize them. The mother country euphemism of "second class citizenship" is a smokescreen that seeks to obscure the colonial status of black people in America.

Viewed on the international plane, integration represents an attempt by the white mother country to forestall the drive for national liberation by its colonial subjects in precisely the same manner as France sought to hold onto its colonial spoils by defining its colonial holdings as "overseas provinces," or as Britain tried to do with its Commonwealth, or as Portugal tried to do with its "overseas provinces." France, England and Portugal have all failed in their attempts to hold onto their colonial possessions by trying to get the colonial subjects themselves to stop short of taking complete sovereignty in their drive for a better life. And so is America doomed to failure in this respect.

In fact, America's failure is even more obscene and contemptible because, as often happens to exploiters, it has believed its own propaganda, its own lies, and it has taken all its perverted deceptions for reality. It is safe to say that so deeply has America submerged itself in mendacity and hypocrisy that it no longer knows what the truth is. So that when someone like Malcolm X, Stokely Carmichael or Rap Brown comes along and utters the bitter truth, America can only deal with them by tagging them "subversives"!

Until Detroit, America refused absolutely to even consider the true nature of the domestic crisis. But Detroit forced a confrontation with the facts through sheer military necessity: President Johnson was forced to place the problem in the hands of the Pentagon so that a war of suppression could be properly carried out by the same entity charged with carrying out the war of suppression against the national liberation struggle in

Vietnam. But even after Detroit, after the shooting stopped, the minions of the power structure returned to their old, hackneyed rhetoric, as though integration were still the operating slogan in the black colony.

Detroit was part of the black colony's land hang-up. The other side of the hang-up is a deep land hunger in the heart of Afro-America. It has always been there, just as much so as in any other people. To even waste time asserting this factor is to yield to racism, to argue with the racist assertion that blacks just aren't like other people. Suffice it to say that Afro-Americans are just as land hungry as were the Mau Mau, the Chinese people, the Cuban people; just as much so as all the people of the world who are grappling with the tyrant of colonialism now, trying to get possession of some land of their own. Even the U.S. government once recognized that black people must have some land, because after the Civil War, black people were promised forty acres and a mule. And Booker T. Washington, the first colonial puppet dictator set up over Afro-America by Imperial America, promised to lead black people, like Moses leading his Zionists, into possession of some land.

When he projected his program for black people some fifty years ago, Marcus Garvey tapped black land hunger by claiming the continent of Africa for black people and reasserting black identification with an ancestral homeland. This marked a major, historic shift in the psyche of black people. It got them over a crucial hump in their struggle up from the white light of slavery into knowledge of themselves and their past. Marcus Garvey gave the ultimate statement of black identity. He went directly to its root, and in doing so he gave black people a firm foundation on which to build.

Marcus Garvey may have solved the universal land question for black people, but he did not solve the specific question of Afro-America and its immediate relationship to the land beneath her feet. The practical prospect of Garvey's actually physically transporting blacks back to Africa turned most black people off because of a world situation and balance of power that made such a solution impossible. And as Garvey's fleet of ships, the Black Star Line, which was supposed to provide transportation for blacks back to Africa, sank in the quicksand set at his feet by the white racist power structure and the bootlickers of his era, Afro-America's land hunger became more acute, more desperate.

Learning from Garvey's failure, Elijah Muhammed knew that he had to deal with Afro-America's land hunger, but he also knew that it would be tactically wise for him to be a little more abstract, in order to more closely approximate the true historical relationship of Afro-Americans to the land beneath their feet. He therefore was very careful never to identify any specific geographical location when he issued his call for land for Afro-America. "We must have some land! Some land of our own, or else!" is the way Elijah Muhammed posed the land question to his people. And it is a fact that black Americans could relate to that particular formulation. It stirred very deeply the land hunger of black people.

However, there is something inadequate, something lacking in that particular slogan, because in practice it impeded rather than enhanced movement. In the first place, it is merely a protest slogan; there is nothing revolutionary about it, because it is asking the oppressor to make a gift to black people. The oppressor is not about to give niggers a damn thing. Black people know this from bitter experience. In a land where the racist pigs of the power structure are doing every dirty thing they can to cut off welfare payments, where they refuse medical care to sick people, where they deliberately deprive black people of education, and where they leave black babies to die from lack of milk, no black person in his right mind is going to stand around waiting for those same pigs to give up some of this land, say five or six states!

But black people waited. They awaited a revolutionary formulation that would be suited to their relationship to America. Stokely Carmichael provided this formulation with his thesis of Black Power. The ingeniousness of this slogan derives precisely from a clear understanding of Afro-American history and a clear perception of the relationship of black people to the land.

Black Power as a slogan does not attempt to answer the land question. It does not deny the existence of that question, but rather very frankly states that at the present moment the land question cannot be dealt with, that black people must put first things first, that there are a few things that must be done before we can deal with the land question. Like, we must first get some power so that we will then be in a position to *force* a settlement of the land question. After black people put themselves, through revolutionary struggle, into a position from which they are able to inflict a political consequence upon America, to hit them where it hurts, then the land question can be brought out.

At a rally in Roxbury, the black colonial enclave of Boston, Massachusetts, Stokely Carmichael told an enthusiastic throng of four thousand blacks: "We are poor, we have no money, but we don't have to pay for the land—we already own it; we paid for it with four hundred years of our sweat, our blood, and our suffering . . . We need a revolution so we can live like proud human beings. Our revolution is for land and until we take the land we are gonna stay poor. If you're poor and if you're black, you've got no rights. We want a redistribution of wealth in this country. We don't want any handouts." Meanwhile, let's get some guns, organize and square off to deal with this honkie.

It can be said that Stokely Carmichael has made a contribution of historic proportions to the national liberation struggle of Afro-America by hurling forth the thesis of Black Power. The only things comparable to it in Afro-American history are the universal slave cry of "Freedom!" and Marcus Garvey's demand of "Africa for the Africans at home and abroad."

In his book, *Home,* LeRoi Jones makes a very acute observation on the contribution of Malcolm X. Says Jones, "The point is that Malcolm had begun to call for Black National Consciousness. And moved this consciousness into the broadest possible arena, operating with it as of now. We do not want a Nation, we are a Nation. We must strengthen and formalize, and play the world's game with what we have, from where we are, as a *truly* separate people" (p. 239).

The necessity upon Afro-America is to move, now, to begin functioning as a nation, to assume its sovereignty, to demand that that sovereignty be recognized by other nations of the world. Stokely Carmichael was received in Havana as a representative of a people, of a Nation, and, in principle, the assembled revolutionaries were recognizing the sovereignty of Afro-America. This lesson was first driven home to Afro-America through Malcolm X's trips to Africa, on which he was received by heads of state as an ambassador of Afro-America.

Even further, more meaningful recognition was given when Malcolm was granted leave to speak for Afro-America before the annual meeting of the Organization of African Unity. Functioning as of now is what black people now know they must do. This is precisely what the slogan Black Power does. That is why it is the first truly revolutionary breakthrough since Marcus Garvey.

Black Power must be viewed as a projection of sovereignty, an embryonic sovereignty that black people can focus on and through which they can make distinctions between themselves and others, between themselves and their enemies—in short, between the white mother country of America and the black colony dispersed throughout the continent on absentee-owned land, making Afro-America a decentralized colony. Black Power says to black people that it is possible for them to build a national organization on somebody else's land.

The parallel between the situation of the Jews at the time of the coming of Theodore Herzl and the present situation of black people in America is fascinating. The Jews had no homeland and were dispersed around the world, cooped up in the ghettos of Europe. Functionally, a return to Israel seemed as impractical as obtaining a homeland for Afro-America now seems. Renowned Jewish leaders were seriously considering transporting the Jews to Argentina, en masse, and developing a homeland there. Others seriously considered obtaining from England the territory of Uganda in East Africa for the same purpose.

The gravitational center of the Jewish population at

that time was in Eastern Europe. With the outbreak of massive pogroms in that area near the end of the nineteenth century, the Jewish people were prepared psychologically to take desperate and unprecedented action. They saw themselves faced with an immediate disastrous situation. Genocide was staring them in the face and this common threat galvanized them into common action.

Psychologically, black people in America have precisely the same outlook as the Jews had then, and they are therefore prepared to take common action for the solution to a common problem. Oppressed because of the color of their skin, black people are reacting on that basis. A nationalist consciousness has at last awakened among the black masses of Afro-America. One would have to search far and wide in the annals of history to find a case where such a tide of nationalism did not continue to sweep the people forward into nationhood—by any means necessary. Given the confusion in America over the distinction between the white mother country and the black colony, and the rapidly developing national consciousness of Afro-America, it is easy to see that unless these titanic forces are harnessed and channelled into creative outlets, such as some of those proposed by black revolutionaries, America is headed for a catastrophe of unprecedented proportions.

The facts of history show that the Jews were able to do precisely the same thing that Afro-America must now do. When Theodore Herzl founded the National Jewish Congress, he virtually founded a government in exile for a people in exile. They would build their organization, their government, and then later on they would get some land and set the government and the people down on the land, like placing one's hat on top of one's head. The Jews did it. It worked. So now Afro-Americans must do the same thing.

In fact, when he moved to found the organization of Afro-American Unity, this is precisely what Malcolm X was doing, founding a government in exile for a people in exile. Stokely Carmichael and Rap Brown are now speaking in the name of that sovereignty, in the name of a Nation. "I am not bound by the laws or the morals of America!" Rap Brown stated in Newark, New Jersey. And in California, the Black Panther Party has begun calling for U.N. membership for Afro-America.

Another proposal of the Black Panthers which is winning more and more support in the black colony is the call for a U.N. supervised plebiscite in black communities across the nation. The purpose of the plebiscite is to answer the question, once and for all: just what the masses of black people want. Do the masses of black people consider themselves a nation? Do they want U.N. membership? The viability of this proposal consists in the fact that it does not call for a response beyond the means of black people. All they are asked to do is answer yes or no—which is about all they can do in America. The proposal avoids the pitfall that proved so disastrous to black nationalism in the past: calling for a response from the black masses that they were unable to give, and offering a solution that could not be delivered.

In the case of Marcus Garvey, the solution was to go back to Africa, but Garvey was unable to program this return home. Knowing this, black people were not able to respond as Garvey dreamed and hoped they would. The same was true of Elijah Muhammad and his call for America to give part of America to black people. But there is nothing unrealistic about the Black Panthers' call for a U.N. supervised plebiscite in the ghettos. The mere widespread agitation for such a plebiscite will create a major crisis for U.S. imperialism. Internationally, America's enemies can be counted upon, in some cases, to endorse the proposal. In other cases, countries that are not willing to go all the way with the idea of a plebiscite will at least give an equivocal response.

Domestically, America will be placed in the peculiar position of arguing to black people that they do not need U.N. membership because they are American citizens. The blacks in the ghettos will respond with, Oh yeah? Well, if I'm an American citizen, why am I treated like a dog? The entire problem will be decisively internationalized and raised to a higher level of debate. The forces of reaction will be placed squarely on the defensive and it will be obvious to all that fundamental changes in the status of black people in America can no longer be postponed or avoided.

So we are now engaged openly in a war for the national liberation of Afro-America from colonial bondage to the white mother country. In our epoch, guerrilla warfare is the vehicle for national liberation all around the world. That it would soon come to America could have been predicted. The spirit has always been there. Only the racist under-estimation of the humanity of black people has blinded America to the potential for revolutionary violence of Afro-America. Nat Turner, Gabriel Prosser and Denmark Vesey, black men who led the most successful slave rebellions in North America, are the spiritual fathers of today's urban guerrillas.

Robert Williams and Malcolm X stand as two titans, even prophetic figures, who heralded the coming of the gun, the day of the gun, and the resort to armed struggle by Afro-America. The fate of these two prophetic figures is of paramount interest: Robert Williams actually picked up the gun against the racist cops of North Carolina, while Malcolm X did not actually pick up the gun but spread the word to an audience that Robert Williams never reached. Malcolm X caused the power structure more public concern than Williams ever did, but in the cloak and dagger world of the CIA and the FBI, Williams has made just as much impact as Malcolm, because Williams hurled a challenge at both the white mother country and the black colony: let the issue be settled by war, let the black colony take up arms against the mother country!

Today Malcolm X is dead and Robert Williams is still alive. Now in China, the guest of the Prophet of the Gun, Mao Tse-tung, Williams is coming into his own because his people have at last risen to his level of consciousness and are now ready for his style of leadership.

The black urban guerrillas already have accepted Williams' challenge. The white power structure, when LBJ handed the black colonial problem over to the tender mercies of the Department of Defense, also served warning that it would meet Williams' challenge blow for blow, in open military terms. Black urban guerrillas now dream of liberating black communities with the gun by eliminating America's police power over black people, i.e., by breaking the power of the mother country over the black colony.

The dream is to bring Robert Williams home. Black

people know that they will not have achieved success in this goal until they can say, Bring Robert Williams home and guarantee him safe conduct, until Williams can stand up in the center of Harlem and deliver a speech and the black people prevent the troops of the occupying Army from coming in and taking him prisoner. Rap Brown and Stokely Carmichael, for instance, must be able to speak before any audience of assembled black people without fear of arrest by the gestapo of the mother country.

In order to bring this situation about, black men know that they must pick up the gun, they must arm black people to the teeth, they must organize an army and confront the mother country with a most drastic consequence if she attempts to assert police power over the colony. If the white mother country is to have victory over the black colony, it is the duty of black revolutionaries to insure that the Imperialists receive no more than a Pyrrhic victory, written in the blood of what America might have become.

April/May, 1968

THE DEATH OF
MARTIN LUTHER KING:
REQUIEM FOR
NONVIOLENCE

The murder of Dr. Martin Luther King came as a surprise—and surprisingly it also came as a shock. Many people, particularly those in the black community who long ago abandoned nonviolence and opted to implement the slogan of Malcolm X—"black liberation by any means necessary"—have been expecting to hear of Dr. King's death for a long time. Many even became tired of waiting. But that Dr. King would have to die was a certainty. For here was a man who refused to abandon the philosophy and the principle of nonviolence in face of a hostile and racist nation which has made it indisputably clear that it has no intention and no desire to grant a redress of the grievances of the black colonial subjects who are held in bondage.

To black militants, Dr. King represented a stubborn and persistent stumbling block in the path of the methods that had to be implemented to bring about a revolution in the present situation. And so, therefore, much hatred, much venom and much criticism was focused upon Dr. King by the black militants. And the contradiction in which he was caught up cast him in the role of one who was hated and held in contempt, both by the whites in America who did not want to free black people, and by black people who recognized the attitude of white America and who wanted to be rid of the self-deceiving doctrine of nonviolence. Still, black militants were willing to sit back and watch, and allow Dr. King to play out his role. And his role has now been played out.

The assassin's bullet not only killed Dr. King, it killed a period of history. It killed a hope, and it killed a dream.

That white America could produce the assassin of Dr. Martin Luther King is looked upon by black people—and not just those identified as black militants—as a final repudiation by white America of any hope of reconciliation, of any hope of change by peaceful and nonviolent means. So that it becomes clear that the only way for black people in this country to get the things that they want—and the things that they have a right to and that they deserve—is to meet fire with fire.

In the last few months, while Dr. King was trying to build support for his projected poor people's march on Washington, he already resembled something of a dead man. Of a dead symbol, one might say more correctly. Hated on both sides, denounced on both sides—yet he persisted. And now his blood has been spilled. The death of Dr. King signals the end of an era and the beginning of a terrible and bloody chapter that may remain unwritten, because there may be no scribe left to capture on paper the holocaust to come.

That there is a holocaust coming I have no doubt at all. I have been talking to people around the country by telephone—people intimately involved in the black liberation struggle—and their reaction to Dr. King's murder has been unanimous: the war has begun. The violent phase of the black liberation struggle is here, and it will spread. From that shot, from that blood. America will be painted red. Dead bodies will litter the streets and the scenes will be reminiscent of the disgusting, terrifying, nightmarish news reports coming out of Algeria during the height of the general violence right before the final breakdown of the French colonial regime.

America has said "No" to the black man's demand for liberation, and this "No" is unacceptable to black people. They are going to strike back, they are going to reply to the escalation of this racist government, this racist society. They are going to escalate their retaliation. And the responsibility for all this blood, for all this death, for all this suffering . . . well, it's beyond the stage of assigning blame. Black people are no longer interested in adjudicating the situation, in negotiating the situation, in arbitrating the situation. Their only interest now is in being able to summon up whatever it will take to wreak the havoc upon Babylon that will force Babylon to let the black people go. For all other avenues have been closed.

The assassin's bullet which struck down Dr. King closed a door that to the majority of black people seemed closed long ago. To many of us it was clear that that door had never been open. But we were willing to allow the hopeful others to bang upon that door for entry, we were willing to sit back and let them do this. Indeed, we had no other choice. But now all black people in America have become Black Panthers in spirit. There will, of course, be those who stand up before the masses and echo the eloquent pleas of Dr. King for a continuation of the nonviolent tactic. They will be listened to by many, but from another perspective: people will look back upon Dr. King and upon his successors with something of the emotions one feels when one looks upon the corpse of a loved one. But it is all dead now. It's all dead now. Now there is the gun and the bomb, dynamite and the knife, and they will be used liberally in America. America will bleed. America will suffer.

And it is strange to see how, with each significant shot that is fired, time is speeded up. How the dreadful days that we all somehow knew were coming seem to cascade down upon us immediately, and the dreadful hours that we thought were years away are immediately upon us, immediately before us. And all eternity is gone, blown away, washed away in the blood of martyrs.

Is the death of Dr. King a sad day for America? No. It is a day consistent with what America demands by its actions. The death of Dr. King was not a tragedy for America. America should be happy that Dr. King is dead, because America worked so hard to bring it about. And now all the hypocritical, vicious madmen who pollute the government of this country and who befoul the police agencies of this country, all of the hypocritical public announcements following the death of Dr. King are being repudiated and held in contempt, not only by black people but by millions of white people who know that had these same treacherous, political gangsters made the moves that clearly lay within their power to make, Dr. King would not be dead, nonviolence would prevail and the terror would not be upon us. These people, the police departments, the legislatures, the government, the Democratic Party, the Republican Party, those commonly referred to as the Establishment or the power structure, they can be looked upon as immediate targets and symbols of blame.

But it has been said that a people or a country gets the leaders and the government that it deserves. And here we have at the death of Dr. King a President by the name of Lyndon Baines Johnson who has the audacity to stand before this nation and mourn Dr. King and to praise his leadership and the nonviolence he espoused, while he has the blood of hundreds of thousands of people and the slaughtered conscience of America upon his hands. If any one man could be singled out as bearing responsibility for bringing about the bloodshed and violence to come, it would be Lyndon Baines Johnson. But not just Lyndon Baines Johnson. All of the greedy, profit-seeking businessmen in America, all of the conniving, unscrupulous labor leaders of America, all of the unspeakable bootlickers, the big businessmen of the civil rights movement and the average man on the streets who feels hatred instilled in his heart by this vicious and disgusting system—the blame is everywhere and nowhere.

Washington, D.C., is burning. My only thought at that is: I hope Stokely Carmichael survives Washington. Chicago is burning, Detroit is burning and there is fire and the sound of guns from one end of Babylon to the other.

Last night I heard Lyndon Baines Johnson admonishing his people, admonishing black people to turn away from violence, and not to follow the path of the assassins. And of all the corn pone that he spouted forth one thing struck me and I felt insulted by it. He was ringing changes on a famous statement made by Malcolm X in his speech, "The Ballot or the Bullet." Malcolm X had prophesied that if the ballot did not prevail in gaining black people their liberation, then the bullet would be made to prevail. And Lyndon Johnson said last night that he was going to prove to the nation and to the American people that the ballot and not the bullet would prevail. Coming from him, it was a pure insult.

Those of us in the Black Panther Party who have been reading events and looking to the future have said that this will be the Year of the Panther, that this will be the Year of the Black Panther. And now everything that I can see leaves no doubt of that. And now there is Stokely Carmichael, Rap Brown, and above all there is Huey P. Newton. Malcolm X prophesied the coming of the gun, and Huey Newton picked up the gun, and now there is gun against gun. Malcolm X gunned down. Martin Luther King gunned down.

I am trying to put a few words on tape because I was asked to do so by the editor of this magazine, to try to give my thoughts on what the assassination of Dr. King means for the future, what is likely to follow and who is likely to emerge as a new or a prevailing leader of black people. It is hard to put words on this tape because words are no longer relevant. Action is all that counts now. And maybe America will understand that. I doubt it. I think that America is incapable of understanding *anything* relevant to human rights. I think that America has already committed suicide and we who now thrash within its dead body are also dead in part and parcel of the corpse. America is truly a disgusting burden upon this planet. A burden upon all humanity. And if we here in America . . .

April 6, 1968

AFFIDAVIT #2
SHOOT-OUT IN OAKLAND

While dictating his "Requiem for Nonviolence" in the Ramparts *office in San Francisco, Cleaver got a telephone call and drove over to Oakland, leaving the essay in the middle of a sentence. A few hours later he was arrested in the aftermath of the shoot-out with the Oakland police and sent to Vacaville Prison. He wrote Affidavit #2 there as his account of the Oakland incident.*

I think that the so-called shoot-out on 28th Street was the direct result of frantic attempts by the Oakland Police Department to sabotage the Black Community Barbecue Picnic, which the Black Panther Party had set up for April 7th in DeFremery Park. The shoot-out occurred the night before the scheduled picnic. We had been advertising the barbecue picnic over the radio (KDIA & KSOL) and we had leafleted the community very heavily and put up many posters, inviting the community to come out and share in the picnic. Also, members of the Black Panther Party had been driving all over East and West Oakland in a sound truck, for a week, telling the people about the picnic and inviting them to come out.

The barbecue picnic was a fund raiser for the Black Panther Party Campaign Fund and for the Huey P. Newton Defense Fund. We were uptight for funds for both of these operations. We were running three candidates for public office: Huey P. Newton for Congress in the 7th Congressional District of Alameda County; Bobby Seale for the 17th Assembly District seat in Alameda County; and Kathleen Cleaver for the 18th Assembly District seat in San Francisco. These campaigns were being run on less than a shoestring, and we came up with the idea of the barbecue picnic hoping to raise a little money. And, of course, there was a constant need of funds for Huey's defense.

We knew that the Oakland Police Department was against the picnic because at first they tried to block clearance when we sought it from the park authorities to hold the picnic at DeFremery Park. They failed in that, but they did succeed in getting the park authorities to impose a lot of ridiculous and crippling rules upon us, such as no speeches at the park, no sound equipment, no passing out of campaign literature, etc. Also, there was constant harassment of the brothers and sisters who were operating the sound truck, and members of the Oakland Police Department had been very active in tearing down the posters we put up to advertise the picnic, just as they had been tearing down the posters we put up to advertise Huey and Bobby's political campaigns. Oakland police were also stopping and harassing party members whom they observed putting up these posters or passing out leaflets. We had invested about $300 in the picnic, so we were anxious for it to come off successfully and without incident.

We had noticed that whenever we staged a large fund raising event, the Oakland police would move, first, to try to prevent it from happening; then, failing that, they would arrest a lot of party members and drain off whatever money was raised because we would then have to bail these party members out of jail and there were legal fees. We became very aware of this. This became very clear to us when we staged the Huey P. Newton Birthday Benefit Rally at the Oakland Auditorium on February 17. At first the Oakland police tried to refuse us the use of the auditorium on the grounds that such a rally would be a public nuisance and create a dangerous situation. We had to get Attorney John George to go down with us and threaten Mr. Luddekke, who operates the auditorium for the City of Oakland, with a civil suit, before they backed up and agreed to allow us the use of the facility. Even so, within a week after the rally, the Oakland Police Department and the Berkeley Police Department arrested a total of sixteen members of our party, including the notorious incident in which our Chairman, Bobby Seale, and his wife Artie were dragged from their bed in the wee hours of the morning and charged with conspiracy to commit murder. There was a lot of public outcry against the police for this blatant harassment and frameup and that charge was quickly dropped. But what a lot of people don't understand is that it was also very expensive to us. Even though the ridiculous charge was dropped, the real purpose of the cops was achieved successfully: to drain away our funds through exorbitant bails and legal fees.

So, in staging the barbecue picnic, we had this experience in mind, and we had cautioned all party members to be on their best behavior in order to avoid any incidents with the police that would provide a pretext for arrest.

Here I have to bring up the name of Captain Mc-Carthy of the Oakland Police Department, because he is one of the chief instigators within the OPD against the Black Panther Party and he has a special grudge against me. When we were making the preliminary arrangements for the rally at the Oakland Auditorium, Mr. Luddekke kept urging us to get in touch with a Sergeant White of the OPD to discuss matters of security with him. Such a discussion seemed disgusting to us at first so we avoided it, but as the date of the rally drew nearer it was clear that it would be best if the matter were dealt with, so on either February 16th, or 17th, I can't remember which, I called the number given me by Mr. Luddekke, talked to Sergeant White, and made an appointment to meet with him to discuss the subject of security at the auditorium during the rally.

Another member of the Black Panther Party, Mr. Emory Douglass, who is our Revolutionary Artist, accompanied me to this meeting, which was held at the headquarters of the Oakland Police Department. When we arrived there, we were met in the lobby by Sergeant White, who took us in to talk to a Captain McCarthy. Entering the room where Captain McCarthy was waiting, Sergeant White introduced us. Captain McCarthy stuck out his big ham of a hand to shake mine. I declined, to which the captain responded: "What's the matter, you too good to shake my hand or something?"

I replied: "In view of the present relationship between your organization and mine, I think that our shaking hands would be out of order."

The captain stared into my eyes. His were cold and

murder blue, and his fat neck, stuffed inside his shirt and choked with his tie, turned red, the color creeping all the way up from his adam's apple to his face and I could see that it took an effort, or a sense of a more urgent interest, to keep him from throwing us out of his office. I made a mental note then to stay out of this pig's way because he was not likely either to forgive or forget me.

Two months later, this captain, backed up by a phalanx of Oakland cops with shotguns levelled at the ready, tried to kick down the door to St. Augustine's Church on 27th and West Street in Oakland and terrorized one of our meetings. On this raid, the captain brought with him and his pigs a white priest and a black preacher, and he used them to try to cool down Reverend Neil, whose church it was and who would not be cooled down by the pious entreaties of the captain's anointed accomplices. This occurred on April 3, three days before this same captain, this time with an army of pigs, directed the murderous attack upon members of the Black Panther Party in which one party member, Bobby Hutton, was viciously and wantonly shot to death by racist pigs who had long lain in wait for a chance to shed the blood of the Black Panthers.

On the night the pigs murdered Little Bobby, we had all been very busy making last minute arrangements for the barbecue picnic scheduled for the next day. The Brother who owns the Soul Food restaurant next to our office at 41st and Grove Street in Oakland was cooking the meat for us and we were running sisters back and forth between the restaurant, the stores, and David Hilliard's house at 34th and Magnolia Street where we were assembling the supplies for the next day.

The cops had been following our cars around all day long. During the day, several different cop cars, at different times, had parked directly across the street from our office and made no secret of the fact that they were watching us, with ugly pig scowls on their faces, that look that says to a black man, "I don't like you, nigger, and I'm watching you, just waiting for one false move." Increasingly, the cops had been following me around so much that I had learned to ignore them and to go on about my business as though they did not even exist.

A white man in Berkeley, who sympathized with the work that our party was doing and who wanted to help us out, called us up one day and said that he had read in our paper that we needed transportation badly and offered to give us two cars. I know that we got one of the promised cars, a white Ford several years old but in good shape, but I do not know if we ever got the other. This was a big help to us but also a headache, because the car had a Florida license plate and none of the brothers liked to drive it because you would invariably be stopped by the cops, particularly when driving through Oakland, and they would use the Florida license plate as a pretext for stopping the car. It took only a few days for the word to get around amongst the Oakland cops that the Panthers had a white Ford with a Florida license plate, and from then on the car was marked. For this reason, I took the responsibility of using the car most of the time because I had what is considered good I.D.— driver's license, draft card, Social Security card, and a variety of press cards from my job at *Ramparts* magazine. I even had one press card issued to me by the United Nations, guaranteed to slow down the already sluggish mental processes of a pig cop, especially a dumb Oakland pig. Several brothers had been stopped driving this car and the cops put them through all kinds of changes: "Are you from Florida? How long have you been in California?" Once an Oakland cop stopped me in this car, and when he asked me whose car it was I told him that a white man from Florida had given it to the Black Panther Party. This seemed to make him very mad, and he said: "You expect me to believe that story? No white man in his right mind would give the Black Panthers a car."

"Maybe this white man is crazy," I said to him.

Anyway, that's why I started using this car more frequently than any of the others we had available to the party.

It is a rule of our party that no well known member of the party is to be out on the Oakland streets at night unless accompanied by two or more other people, because we felt that if the Oakland cops ever caught one of us alone like that there was a chance that such a one might be killed and there would be only racist pig cops for witnesses: Verdict of the Coroner's Inquest, "Justifiable Homicide." Period. After the way they tried to murder our leader, Minister of Defense Huey P. Newton, we were not taking any chances. So on the night of April 6, the car I was driving was being followed by two carloads of Panthers and I was on my way to David Hilliard's house at 34th and Magnolia. In the car with me were David Hilliard, Wendell Wade, and John Scott, all members of the Black Panther Party.

We were only a few blocks away from David's house when, all of a sudden, I was overcome by an irresistible urge, a necessity, to urinate, and so I turned off the brightly lighted street we were on (I think it was 30th

Street, but I'm not sure, not being overly familiar with the area), pulled to the curb, stopped the car, got out and started relieving myself. The two Panther cars following us pulled up behind to wait. While I was in the middle of this call of nature, a car came around the corner from the direction that we ourselves had come, and I found myself in danger of being embarrassed, I thought, by a passing car. So I cut off the flow, then, and awkwardly hurried around to the other side of the car, to the sidewalk, to finish what had already been started and what was most difficult to stop—I recall that I did soil my trousers somewhat. But this car, instead of passing, stopped, and a spotlight from it was turned on and beamed my way. I could see it was the cops, two of them. They got out of the car and stood there, not leaving the car, each standing just outside. One of them shouted, "Hey, you, walk out into the middle of the street with your hands up, quick!"

For the second time, I had to deal with a ticklish situation and I was so close to the end that I could not resist finishing. I shouted back to the cops, "O.K., O.K.!" I turned, trying to zip up my fly and get out into the middle of the street. Common sense told me that I'd best have my hands up by the time I cleared the front of my car. But before I cleared, the cop on the passenger side of his car started shouting and firing his gun, and then the other cop started shooting. I am not sure they were shooting at me because the lights from their car were shining brightly at me, blocking my vision. But the explosions from their guns sounded right in my face and so, startled, I dove for cover in front of my car. The Panthers in the other two cars started yelling at the cops and honking their horns and getting out of their cars, and the brothers who were in my car scrambled out of the passenger side.

Above my head, the windshield of my car shattered and I looked behind me. There was another cop car at the other end of the street, from which shots were also being fired at us. In fact, shots seemed to be coming from everywhere; it sounded like the entire block had erupted with gunfire. It took only a split second to see that they had us in a cross fire, so I shouted to the brothers, "Scatter! Let's get out of here!" Our best bet, it was clear, was to make it across the street and that's where we headed. As we started across, one of the Panthers, Warren Wells, got hit and let out an agonized yelp of pain as he fell to the ground. I dove for the pavement, in about the middle of the street, with bullets ricocheting off the pavement all around me and whizzing past my head. I was being fired at from several different directions and for the second time within the space of a few minutes I could taste death on my tongue. But I kept crawling across the street as fast as I could and I truthfully didn't know whether I had been hit or not, whether I was dead or dying. I was hurting all over from scraping against the pavement and I was still being shot at. I saw a couple of Panthers run between two houses and got to my feet and followed them. A cop with a shotgun was running after me, shooting. I didn't have a gun but I wished that I had! (O, how I wish that I had!!!)

As I ran between those two houses, I saw a Panther climbing over what looked like a fence. I hit it just as soon as he was over, only to find out, as I climbed up, that it was some sort of a shed and I was on top of it and the cop behind me was still shooting at me with the shotgun. I dove off and onto the ground on the other side, landing on top of Bobby Hutton. Before I had recovered from the jolt of my leap, I was wishing that I had never come over the top of that shed, that I had stayed there to face that cop with that blazing shotgun, because Little Bobby and I were boxed in. The shed at our backs spanned the space between the houses on either side of us, and although the area in front of us was clear all the way out to the street, we could not budge from that little nook because the street was filled with cops and they were pumping shots at us as though shooting was about to go out of style. In the dark, I could not see that Little Bobby had a rifle, until it started to bark, producing a miraculous effect: the cops, cowardly pigs from their flat feet to their thick heads, all ran for cover. The few seconds that this gave us allowed us to find a door into the basement of the house to our right, and we dove inside. We were just in time to escape a murderous fusillade of shots that scoured the tiny area we had just abandoned.

But if jumping over the shed had been like going from the frying pan into the fire, entering that house defies description. The walls were like tissue paper and the pigs were shooting through them from all four sides at once. It was like being the Indians in all the cowboy movies I had ever seen. What saved us for the moment was an eighteen-inch-high cement foundation running around the cellar at the base of the wall. We lay down flat against the floor while the bullets ripped through the walls. This unrelenting fire went on for about half an hour, and then it stopped and the pigs started lobbing in tear gas. While the gas was being pumped in through the windows, Little Bobby and I took the opportunity to fortify the walls with whatever we could lay our hands on: furniture, tin cans, cardboard boxes —it was hopeless but we tried it anyway. While I was standing up trying to move a thick board over against the wall, I was struck in the chest by a tear gas cannister fired through a window. It knocked me down and almost out. Little Bobby, weak from the gas, was coughing and choking, but he took all my clothes off in an effort to locate a wound in the dark, patting me down for the moist feel of blood.

The pigs started shooting again and we had to hit the deck. The material we had stacked along the wall was blown away by what sounded like machine gun fire. We decided to stay in there and choke to death if necessary rather than walk out into a hail of bullets. Above the din of gunfire, we could hear the voices of people yelling at the cops to stop shooting, calling them murderers and all kinds of names, and this gave us the strength and the hope to hang on. The tear gas was not as hard to endure as I had imagined it to be. My lungs were on fire, nose and eyes burning, but after a while I couldn't feel anything. Once Little Bobby told me he was about to pass out. He did, but he came to before long, and the two of us lay there counting the minutes and ducking the bullets that were too numerous to count. One of the shots found my leg and my foot with an impact so painful and heavy that I was sure I no longer had two legs. But it didn't seem to matter because I was also sure that it was only a matter of seconds before one of the bullets found a more vital spot. In my mind, I was actually saying good-bye to the world and I was sure that Little Bobby was doing the same thing. Lying there pinned down like that, there was nothing else to do. If there was I couldn't think of it. I said goodbye to my wife, and an image of her dancing for me, as I had watched her do so' many times before, floated past my mind's eye, and I reached out to touch her, to kiss her goodbye with my fingers. Then my mind seemed to dwell on crowds of people, masses of people, millions of people, as though the whole human race, all the men and women who had ever lived, seemed to present themselves to my view. I saw images of parades, crowd scenes in auditoriums. I remembered the people at the rally in the Oakland Auditorium, the surging, twisting sea of people at the Peace and Freedom Party Convention at the Richmond Auditorium; these two events somehow coupled in my mind. I saw throngs of students at Merritt College, at San Francisco State College, and at UC Berkeley, and then I heard Little Bobby ask me, "What are we going to do?"

I felt an impotent rage at myself because all I could tell him was to keep his head down, that head with its beautiful black face which I would watch a little later, again powerless, as the mad dogs outside blasted him into eternity. Was it in cold blood? It was in the coldest of blood. It was murder. MURDER! And that must never be forgotten: the Oakland Police Department MURDERED Little Bobby, and they cannot have that as a victory. Every pig on that murderous police force is guilty of murdering Little Bobby; and lying, hypocritical Chief Gains is Murderer No. 1. And we must all swear by Little Bobby's blood that we will not rest until Chief Gains is brought to justice, either in the courts or in the streets; and until the bloodthirsty troops of the Oakland Police Department no longer exist in the role of an occupying army with its boots on the neck of the black community, with its guns aimed at the black community's head, an evil force with its sword of terror thrust into the heart of the black community. That's what Little Bobby would ask you to do, Brothers and Sisters, put an end to the terror—by any means necessary. All he asks, all Huey asks, all I ask, is what Che Guevera asked:

> *Wherever Death may surprise us*
> *It will be welcome, provided that*
> *This, our battle cry, reach some*
> *Receptive ear; that another hand*
> *Reach out to pick up the gun, that*
> *Other fighting men come forward*
> *To intone our funeral dirge*
> *To the staccato of machine gun fire*
> *And new cries of battle and victory.*

The rest of the story is madness, pain, and humiliation at the hands of the Pigs. They shot firebombs into the cellar, turning it into a raging inferno, and we could not stand the heat, could not breathe the hot air with lungs already raw from the tear gas. We had to get out of there, to flee from certain death to face whatever awaited us outside. I called out to the Pigs and told them that we were coming out. They said to throw out the guns. I was lying beneath a window, so Little Bobby passed me the rifle and I threw it outside, still lying on my back. Then Little Bobby helped me to my feet and we tumbled through the door. There were pigs in the windows above us in the house next door, with guns pointed at us. They told us not to move, to raise our hands. This we did, and an army of pigs ran up from the street. They started kicking and cursing us, but we were already beyond any pain, beyond feeling. The pigs told us to stand up. Little Bobby helped me to my feet. The pigs pointed to a squad car parked in the middle of the street and told us to run to it. I told them that I couldn't run. Then they snatched Little Bobby away from me and shoved him forward, telling him to run to the car. It was a sickening sight. Little Bobby, coughing and choking on the night air that was burning his lungs as my own were burning from the tear gas, stumbled forward as best he could, and after he had traveled about ten yards the pigs cut loose on him with their guns, and then they turned to me. But before they could get into anything, the black people in the neighborhood who had been drawn to the site by the gunfire and commotion began yelling at them, calling the pigs murderers, telling them to leave me alone. And a face I will never forget, the face of the captain with the murder blue eyes, loomed up.

"Where are you wounded?" he asked me.

I pointed out my wound to him. The Pig of Pigs looked down at my wound, raised his foot and stomped on the wound.

"Get him out of here," he told the other pigs, and they took me away.

Why am I alive? While at Highland Hospital, a pig said to me: "You ain't going to be at no barbecue picnic tomorrow. You the barbecue now!" Why did Little Bobby die? It was not a miracle, it just happened that way. I know my duty. Having been spared my life, I don't want it. I give it back to our struggle. Eldridge Cleaver died in that house on 28th Street, with Little

Bobby, and what's left is force: fuel for the fire that will rage across the face of this racist country and either purge it of its evil or turn it into ashes. I say this for Little Bobby, for Eldridge Cleaver who died that night, for every black man, woman, and child who ever died here in Babylon, and I say it to racist America, that if every voice of dissent is silenced by your guns, by your courts, by your gas chambers, by your money, you will know, that as long as the ghost of Eldridge Cleaver is afoot, you have an ENEMY in your midst.

April 19, 1968

OPEN LETTER

TO RONALD REAGAN

California Medical Facility
Vacaville, California
May 13, 1968

The Honorable Ronald Reagan
Governor of the State of California
Sacramento, California

Honorable Sir:

In writing you this letter, I want first of all to make one thing clear: I do not write it to ask a favor of you; I do not write it seeking mercy; I do not write it to complain. Rather, I am writing to you to call to your attention that certain persons who are responsible to you have conspired to violate my rights and are now holding me as a political prisoner at Vacaville Medical Facility, one of the chain of prisons operated by the California Department of Corrections, a state agency, under your control. As the Chief Executive of the State of California, I thought you might want to know what the people whom you have appointed to the California Adult Authority have done. And whether you in fact want to know about it or not, as the Chief Executive it is your duty to see to it that the agencies under your control carry out their functions in such a manner as not to violate the rights of any citizen of the State of California, or of any other state or jurisdiction, for that matter. I want to speak to you about a clear instance in which my rights have been violated in a most flagrant and indefensible manner. So it is from that point of view that I write this letter, and it is in that spirit that I hope you will receive it, look into the matter, and then act, or not act, as your reason, conscience, and advisors move you.

I am a political prisoner, and an examination of the circumstances resulting in my imprisonment will reveal this fact to you or to anybody else. I realize that I have just asserted an awkward claim, because I know that other people have already examined the circumstances of which I speak and have drawn the conclusion that, indeed, I should be right where I am. But I do not intend to argue their side of the story, which I not only consider wrong, but perfidious and criminal. Because certain people had to do certain things in order for me to be, at this moment, sitting in this cell. People talked about me and my activities and then they issued orders. Other people moved to carry out those orders. Those who fastened the handcuffs to my wrists, the shackles around my legs, the chain around my body, put me into a car, transported me to this place and turned me over to the keepers here, were mere functionaries, automatons, carrying out their "duties" in Adolf Eichmann's spirit. I speak, rather, of the decision makers, those whom you have appointed and charged with making decisions in this area. They are the guilty ones, the conspirators, whose decisions and orders I bring to your attention.

I was on parole in San Francisco, after serving nine years of a fourteen-year sentence in San Quentin, Folsom, and Soledad. I was released on December 12, 1966. My parole agent was Mr. R. L. Bilideau. I was given four years' parole by the California Adult Authority, presumably because, according to their lights, I had been rehabilitated. According to my own lights, I had.

Having gone to prison from Los Angeles, I decided to take my parole to San Francisco, to start anew in a brand new locale, there to stand or fall on my own merit, and to build a brand new life. I did this with ease, with a thirst for life, a driving hunger to be involved in life, the real life that I had watched for so long from the sidelines of a stagnant, deadening, artificial world. I found love, and married it. Her name is Kathleen, my darling wife. While in prison I decided that, upon my release, I would find a way to relate to the struggle of my people for a better life, to plunge myself into that struggle and contribute of myself what I possessed that could be used, without reservation: my life, my fortune, and my sacred honor which, through my struggles to survive the soul-murder of my stay in prison, I found.

After a few false starts, I encountered the Black Panther Party, which I quickly joined, and after proving myself, was appointed to the position of Minister of Information. It is a position which I still hold and of which I am as proud, Governor, as I imagine you are of the office you hold. You may have heard of my party, and I certainly have heard of yours. We visited you in Sacramento last year on May 2nd, and, if I may say so, were very badly received. As I understand it, this was because some of us brought our guns with us, even though your men had theirs with them. Morever, your men turned their guns on us, although we did not do the same thing to them. We were told that your men had the right to have their guns but that ours didn't. We argued the point, of course, but evidently our arguments fell on deaf ears, because our men with guns were arrested and some of them had to serve a jail sentence. I was arrested also, but quickly released with all charges dropped. Then a judge discovered that I should not have been arrested in the first place because I was there as a reporter, with proper credentials, for *Ramparts* magazine, of which I was then and still am, a staff writer; because I did not have a gun; and because, in reference to my being on parole, I had the written consent of my parole agent to be there. That was the only time in my eighteen months on parole that I was ever arrested. Since that situation was resolved as it was, I think it would be fair to say, Governor, that in those eighteen months I was never arrested for cause.

If the truth were to be told, I was a model parolee, although I gather that I was something of a headache to my parole agent. This was through no fault of my own, but because he was caught up in the contradiction between the presumptions of the parole department and my human rights and my Constitutional rights to engage in political activity. He was always telling me that, although I had a perfect right to be a Black Panther, there were politicians in Sacramento who did not approve of the party. It was his advice that if I wanted to be successful on parole, I be cool. *Be cool?* For nine long years I had been on *ice*. Shit. I was being cool. In fact I was still thawing out, trying to warm up, so that I could really do my thing. Besides, legality was on my side. As for politicians, I was one myself. (I guess I forgot that politics, especially when they start to get deep, get dirty. You can't really count on anything, not even, as in my own case, the Constitution of the United States. Still, I was not *really* counting on that, being aware as I was that some politicians, in the name of upholding the Constitution, violate it, yea, rub it in the mud.)

But I am Minister of Information of the Black Panther Party. And what would be the quality of my soul, politics, and value to my party, to my comrades, and to the people we represent, if (through mere fear of hostile politicians) I abdicated the responsibilities I had accepted and pledged myself to fulfill? Having yourself taken an oath of office, Governor, I'm sure you can understand that. Suppose Jesse Unruh sent you a threatening message demanding that you resign as governor. I know what you would do: you would tell Big Daddy where to go. Well, I did more or less the same thing, but that was, at least it was *supposed* to be, just between me and my parole agent. I chose to stick to my guns. Anyway, I thought that the politicians in Sacramento had better things to do than to be fucking around with parolees, and the party didn't have any plans for visiting the State Capital again. Dispensing information seemed innocuous enough, and besides, I was so busy that I didn't have much time to worry about it.

Huey P. Newton, Minister of Defense of the Black Panther Party, was uptight, on Death Row, and he needed me: District Attorney Coakley of Alameda County was prosecuting my leader for murder, in the name of the People of the State of California, so it was very clear to me that the people needed some information they didn't seem to have: about Huey, about the Black Panther Party, about the Oakland Police Department, about District Attorney Coakley, about black people, about 1968, about the black response to white racism (this was before LBJ decided to give me a hand by issuing his Civil Disorders Report), and about politics—and about how all that jazz was mixed up, interrelated with welfare, police brutality, bad housing, the war in Vietnam—all that shit. All that shit had to be put into a perspective from which the people could see, and understand, and join in the demand that Huey Must Be Set Free! Come See About Huey!

Whew! To tell you the truth, Governor, that shit was wearing me out. I was getting old before my time: I'm twenty-two years old, the age I was when I went to prison, because when I got out, there was a great big gap in my soul that had to be filled. I filled it with the Black Revolution. In practical terms, I filled it with Huey, because Huey is the incarnation of the Black Revolution, if you can dig that.

And then along came the Peace and Freedom Party. Politics. What the hell. We had called them, hadn't we? "Come See About Huey, but the rest of you don't come." No, we were serious, and there was very little time. The Black Revolution was at stake, and we needed every hand we could get, because the people needed information.

O.K. We had asked for it, and here it was: the Peace and Freedom Party. Politics. How do we relate to it? Shit. Do you think we had a hard time coming up with the answer, Governor? If you do, you are as wrong as two left shoes, because it was as simple as "States' Rights" is to George Wallace. He, by the way, came along with his National States' Rights Party, the American Independence Party, at the same time as the Peace and Freedom Party, as I'm sure you are aware. But they didn't come to see about Huey. I think they went to see about the Oakland Police Department and D. A. Coakley. The Peace and Freedom people only needed a little information because they already had a lot of their own. In fact, it would be fair to say that we exchanged information with them. After that, it was just a question of apportioning the work load, which we did, at the Richmond Auditorium, at the Founding Convention of the Peace and Freedom Party. That was in March, and a grand coalition was formed between Browns (Brown Caucus), Whites (White Caucus), and Blacks (Black Caucus)—that's a little complicated, Governor, I know, but let me leave it like that. If you want more information on that subject, contact the Peace and Freedom people or the Black Panthers or the Mexican-Americans, and they will fill you in. If I could leave here, I would be glad to go get that information for you, because you really should know about it, it's a brand new bag; but this joint I'm in sort of cramps my style. Informationwise.

The notorious, oppressive, racist, and brutal Oakland Police Department is at the heart of the matter. This gestapo force openly and flagrantly terrorizes the black people of Oakland. The Black Panther Party took a position against what the OPD was and is doing to black people. As one of the chief spokesmen for the party, I became well known to the OPD and I was hated by them. I know that they hated me; I've seen murderous hatred burning in their eyes. They hated the whole idea of a Black Panther Party, and they were out to destroy it. We were out, on the other hand, to organize the black community so that it could put an end to the terror. We saw no reason why we shouldn't do this, and nobody else seemed to be doing anything about it. If they were, it was not showing, because things were getting worse and not better. The OPD had increased its patrols of the black community to the saturation point, and become like a sword buried in the heart of the people. The Black Panther Party intended to remove that sword.

In its effort to counter the party's drive, the OPD launched a systematic campaign of harassment by arrest of party members, particularly its leaders. Take a look at the rap sheets of Huey P. Newton, our Minister of Defense, or David Hilliard, our National Captain, or Bobby Seale, our Chairman. You will find a string of phony cases as long as your arm. On October 28, 1967, they attempted to murder Huey, then charged him with murder when one of their own men came up dead. On April 6, 1968, they attempted to murder me, shot me, and did murder a member of our party—Bobby Hutton, seventeen years old. And then they charged me with attempting to murder them!

Governor Reagan, I would call to your attention an old saying: that where there is smoke there is fire; because there is a lot of smoke around the Oakland Police Department. I submit that the smoke is from the frequent use of their guns against the black community. It deserves looking into. As the Governor of the State of California, you would not be stepping out of your place if you looked into Oakland. Besides, it may be easier for you to look into Oakland than for anybody else. I understand that you have many friends and supporters in Oakland and that recently you received a warm welcome by the Republican convention there.

Well, on the night that I was shot and arrested, the OPD came up with the paranoid, fantastic notion that other members of the Black Panther Party *might* invade the jail and rescue me. (Shit. Anybody *might* do anything!) So they got in touch with the California Adult Authority (did they, I wonder, get in touch with you?) and asked them to come get me and take me to San Quentin. The OPD communicated its own panic to the Adult Authority, because at the absurd hour of 4 A.M., Sunday morning, April 7, two of its members (a quorum meeting over the telephone; voices groggy from sleep) ordered my parole revoked and I was taken to San Quentin, and from there to Vacaville. I have at last been served by the Adult Authority with three reasons for revoking my parole. Here they are:

(1) Eldridge Cleaver violated his parole by being in possession of a gun.

(2) Eldridge Cleaver violated his parole by associating with people of bad reputation.

(3) Eldridge Cleaver violated his parole by failing to cooperate with his parole agent.

Are you outraged, Governor? I am, and I think you should be. Let me point out why. On what do they base the first charge? The impeccable word of the Oakland Police Department! (After the Surgeon General of the United States said to stop, after the Chiefs of Police of both San Francisco and Los Angeles issued orders to stop, the OPD still hasn't said that it will stop using mace on the citizens of the state you govern.) This charge by the Adult Authority amounts to nothing more nor less than an invasion into the province of the Judiciary. I have been imprisoned without a trial; I have entered a plea of Not Guilty to the charge in the Superior Court; but the Adult Authority has already convicted and sentenced me. Am I not entitled to a trial?

The second charge—that I associated with people of bad reputation—is fantastic. Now I realize that all black people have a bad reputation in the eyes of certain racists, but the Adult Authority here refers to members of the Black Panther Party. My parole officer, Mr. Bilideau, told me, and I quote him, that "it's all right with us if you are a Black Panther." We had a full discussion of the matter and he merely cautioned me about Sacramento politicians who don't like the Panthers. My question is, in whose opinion does the Black Panther Party have a bad reputation? Certainly not in the opinion of the black community, and not in the opinion of all white people. So what's this shit about reputation? Hundreds of people, all over the Bay Area, all over the state, across the nation, and around the world, have cried out against the persecution of the Black Panther Party by the Oakland Police Department. As a matter of fact, if we are going to speak of reputations, the Oakland Police Department has the worst reputation of any police department in the State of California, and can only be compared to the racist police in Mississippi and South Africa. So what is the Adult Authority doing associating with this disreputable police force? Ah, they have a regular thing going. The prisons of California are bursting with people handed over by the Oakland Police Department. Pure and simple, this bad reputation jazz is nothing but political opinion, uninformed at that.

The third and last charge, that I failed to cooperate with my parole officer, turns my stomach inside out, because it is a lie. Like the other charges, it is an afterthought, conjured up as justification for the precipitous action of ordering me back to prison. (Why is it that when some people see that they have made a serious mistake, instead of moving to correct it and offer relief to the victim of their mistake, they move to fabricate a justification? I know a boxcarful of convicts who are better men than that, who are more than willing to admit that they were wrong.) The last time I saw my parole officer, just a few days before I was arrested, we shook hands, and his parting words to me were: "I want you to do me a favor, Eldridge. When I get a copy of your book, will you autograph it for me?" We both laughed, and I said, "Isn't this a fantastic turn of events? Just think of it: all these years I have been dependent on you guys signing things for me, and now I get a chance to sign something for you! It will be a pleasure!"

I do not know whether or not my parole officer actually submitted such a lying report against me, or whether the Adult Authority merely charged me in his name, because failure to cooperate with one's parole officer is a routine charge lodged against men whose paroles are revoked. It is a cliche, tossed in for good measure. And the Adult Authority operates in such a secret fashion, is cloaked with such an impenetrable shroud of darkness, that nobody knows what goes on in its Star Chamber proceedings. However, if my parole officer did submit that lie, I would be more hurt than surprised, because in my time I have seen enough of the organization men of the Department of Corrections so that nothing they do could surprise me, no matter how nauseating. But you know, Governor, when you have frequent contact with another person for eighteen months, something between you is built up. You get to know each other on a human level, you learn to see

inside each other's personalities, and there are certain
things that human beings naturally expect from each
other, like not to be stabbed in the back. But, alas, it is
not so, or else why and from what depth of a sense of
betrayal, could Caesar say, Et tu Brute? *Et tu Bilideau?*

Well, there you are, Governor, that is more or less
the substance of what I wanted to lay before you. But
permit me to add a few remarks. I am finished with the
California Department of Correction, with the Adult
Authority, with parole officers, with prisons, and all of
their world of restraint, confinement, and punishment.
I can't relate to them anymore, because I am free. I
am a free man, Governor, and I no longer know how to
submit and play the part of a debtor to society. What
I owe to society is the work that I must do outside these
stone walls. My work can't wait, it won't wait, it should
not wait. And you, Governor, should welcome me back
to my job, because I was dealing with some of the most
pressing problems facing not only the State of California but this nation and the world. And the people you
can't reach, the dispossessed and oppressed people—
whom you can't even talk to, whom you can't understand, and who neither trust nor understand you—are
the very people with whom I am on the best of terms,
for I am of them, I am one of them. You and I, Governor, have both been working on the same problems, except that you are working from the top down and I am
working from the bottom up. The bottom of the world
is in motion, Governor, and Bobby Dylan's "empty
handed beggar" is at the door, except that his hand is
not empty any more. He's got a gun in that hand. And
he's stopped begging. In fact, he's nearly stopped talking,
because it's becoming clear to him that hardly anybody

is listening. When he finally stops talking altogether, he is going to start shooting. This brings to a conclusion what I wanted to talk to you about, and I have nothing else to say, except one question: Have you been listening to me, Governor?

Respectfully submitted,
Eldridge Cleaver
Minister of Information
Black Panther Party.

AN ASIDE TO RONALD REAGAN

I have never liked Ronald Reagan. Even back in the days of his bad movies—bullshit flicks that never turned me on to any glow—I felt about him the way I felt about such nonviolent cowboys as Roy Rogers and Gene Autry: that they were never going to cause any action or allow anything to happen. They were just there, occupying space and wasting my time, my money and my sanity. There was a sort of unreality in their style. One knew that movies were into a make-believe bag, but the unreality espoused on the screen by the flat souls of such Pablum-fed actors as Reagan reflected to me—black ghetto nigger me—a sickening mixed bag of humorless laughter and perfect Colgate teeth, with never a hint of the real funk of life. Insipid, promising nothing and delivering even less, a Reagan movie was nothing to get excited about. There would be no surprises.

But what happened was that Ronnie landed a TV show. Equipped with opulent sponsors and some slick script writers, the mediocrity of his grade-B spirit was glossed over and concealed by the make-up of a rhetoric fashioned by a committee of crew-cut wordmongers. With all this going for him, it was natural for him to turn to politics when Hollywood's keenest make-up artists began to find it increasingly difficult to deal with the wrinkles that were slowly turning his face into a replica of well-furrowed, depleted, single-crop soil.

He was in the best of all states to get into his thing; California had demonstrated its ability to relate to the politics of the absurd by electing to office such blobs of political putty as Richard Nixon and Max Rafferty. And having picked the proper place, he could not have chosen a better style. Ronnie used a pat formula that said: pick the toughest problems confronting the people and launch blistering attacks upon all sincere efforts to come to grips with these problems; offer as an alternative a conglomeration of simple-minded cliches and catch phrases that go back to the *Mayflower*; sing the "Star-Spangled Banner" and smile broadly, effusively, as you wave the flag at the people; use a fighting "I'm fed up" form of delivery; and always remember that when nothing else works, there is still the tried and proven gambit of demagogic politicians, especially in California—viciously attack the perennial whipping boys of the American Dream: subversion concealed in the words of textbooks, the "decadence of universities and the misguided students being duped by a handful of professors who are under the subtle influence of the Communist Conspiracy."

Well, it worked. Mickey Mouse is governor and Donald Duck is a candidate for the U.S. Senate. That is what we have to worry about. And deal with.

It has been said that the people get the rulers they deserve. I do not believe, however, that America has the rulers it deserves. The State of California, emphatically, could not deserve the rulers it has. Yet we have them, and this is an election year. And what an election year: this is the nightmare election year of the American Dream.

Everything is out in the open this year. Nobody is trying very hard to conceal anything. As usual, the key issue in the election is what to do about the niggers —only this time, the question is being rewritten to read, what to do *with* the niggers. From the point of view of the niggers themselves, the question has also been rewritten and now reads, what are we going to do about this shit?

A surprising development—one which offers the possibility, perhaps the only possibility, of a monkey wrench being tossed into the smoke dreams of the racists—is that a sizable portion of white Americans are in revolt against the system. So the issue of Law and Order, or Crime in the Streets, becomes key.

In California, Mickey Mouse looked out from his perch in Disneyland for an opening to get himself back into the act, having been kicked off the stage in Miami by a pig who had been in the game a little longer. From where he lurked, Mickey Mouse fixed his blank stare on the campus of the University of California, Berkeley. He had received a tip that a situation tailored to his needs existed on that campus. Eldridge Cleaver—the apotheosis of the American nightmare: loudmouthed nigger, ex-convict, rapist, advocate of violence, Presidential candidate—was retained by the Berkeley subversives to teach a class on the university campus, i.e., to corrupt the morals of lily-white American youth. So Ronnie Baby, doing his Republican duty, emerged from his pen to take up the cudgels of battle: "If Eldridge Cleaver is allowed to teach our children, they may come home some night and slit our throats. Therefore, the *people* of the State of California will not stand for this!"

Right on, Mickey Mouse. There are those of us who know what you are into, and we don't like it. Furthermore, we are going to deal with it, with you, to put an end to your absurd oinking in the faces of the people. So that all those bullshit changes that you went through with the Board of Regents, forcing them to emasculate the course in which I was to participate as a guest lecturer, don't mean shit. It displeased you, I understand, that even the Board of Regents did not buy you whole hog; that, in fact, they agreed to allow me to deliver one lecture.

Big deal. Who in the fuck do you think you are, telling me that I can't talk, telling the students and faculty members at UC Berkeley that they cannot have me deliver ten lectures? I'm going to do it whether you like it or not. In fact, my desire now is to deliver *twenty* lectures. You, Donald Duck Rafferty, Big Mama Unruh, and that admitted member of the racist John Birch Society who introduced that resolution into the legislature to censure those responsible for inviting me to lecture in the first place—all and each of you can kiss my black nigger ass, because I recognize you for what you are, racist demagogues who have their eye on the ballot box come November. The students and the faculty members at Berkeley are trying to salvage the American people from the brink of chaos that you pigs have brought on. Your thirst and greed for power is so great that you don't care whether or not in your lust you destroy the vital processes of a barbaric society that is trying in its parts to become civilized.

I don't know what the outcome of all this will be, but I do know that I, for one, will never kiss your ass, will never submit to your demagogic machinations. I think you are a cowardly, cravenhearted wretch. You are not a man. You are a punk. Since you have insulted me by calling me a racist, I would like to have the opportunity to balance the books. All I ask is a sporting chance. Therefore, Mickey Mouse, I challenge you to a duel, to the death, and you can choose the weapons. And if you can't relate to that, right on. Walk, chicken, with your ass picked clean.

October 26, 1968

STANFORD SPEECH

Soon after Judge Raymond J. Sherwin of the California Superior Court ordered Eldridge Cleaver released on a writ of habeas corpus, Cleaver was offered a teaching position in an experimental sociology course at the University of California. Governor Ronald Reagan hysterically denounced the Cleaver appointment and maneuvered the Regents, the university's governing board, into denying academic credit to students taking the course. Cleaver responded with his "Aside to Reagan," printed in Ramparts, *and with a series of polemical speeches on college campuses throughout the state—of which the following speech, given at Stanford University, is typical.*

Good evening, ladies and gentlemen. I want to thank those who were responsible for inviting me down here, and I want to thank Mickey Mouse Ronald Reagan and Donald Duck Rafferty for making it possible.

I would like to introduce to you the Minister of Education of the Black Panther Party, George Murray. He's the other menace to higher education here in California, a brother that you've heard about and read about, having his job at San Francisco State College, destroying education: George Murray.

It's very difficult to find out just where to start; in the middle, on the side, the front, the top or the bottom. Because when you look at the situation we're confronted with today, from whatever angle you look at it, it's just a lot of bullshit going on. Some people told me when I came down here that I shouldn't use any four-letter words. Because they said this was Stanford University. They said this was not a state-supported institution, this was private money. And when you curse at a state-supported institution, you're cursing part of your own money; you can do that, but this is someone else's money and you've got to have a little respect. I want to couple my basic response to that with my response to Ronald Reagan. I guess people are getting more and more permissive in this society, because I think people are ready to hear someone say Fuck Ronald Reagan, or Fuck the private money at Stanford University. Fuck Stanford University if that's necessary, dig it? That may or may not be the limit of my vocabulary, I don't know. I don't go around counting words. Because we're reaching the point today where words are becoming more and more irrelevant. The brother that introduced me failed to mention the affiliation with the Black Panther Party; but that's the foundation, that's where we start, and it looks like that's where we're going to end, if certain people have their way.

There are rumors going around today that people have lost their spirit, that they can no longer deal with the problems confronting society, that it's necessary to throw up both hands, and allow the professionals like

Nixon, Reagan, and Humphrey and Georgie-boy Wallace to come in and rescue us and to save us and to offer salvation to the people. We think this is another lie, a part of the tissue of lies that everyone in this country's been fed all of their lives, all of the history of this country, and we say that people don't have to submit to lies, that you don't have to tuck tail, when a fool like Ronald Reagan screams at you; that you don't have to do that.

There is such a thing as free will, and it is possible for you to stand up, to let your voice be heard, if you're willing to suffer the consequences. The necessary thing is to take action, to state your position, and if possible, avoid the consequences. Because the consequences being meted out by the power structure today are extreme, very hard to handle, and not something that I would wish onto the head of anyone. Everyone accuses the Black Panther Party of having a police hang-up—the only thing that we can do is sit around, ambush policemen, and call them pigs. Those are just some of the things that we can do. That's not all. That's not all.

It's very important to realize that if we don't have understanding, then we can't gain anything at all. The basic problem in this country today is political confusion. People don't know who their enemies are; they don't know who their friends are. They don't know whether to be afraid of the right or of the left. They don't know whether they themselves belong on the right or on the left, so they just say, Fuck it, throw up both hands, take acid trips, freak out on weed and pills —alcohol is still with us. People feel that they just can't deal with the situation. And that's because, I believe, the people have been consciously manipulated to that end.

We are dealing with a situation where the Democratic Party has lifted its standard bearer, Lyndon Baines Johnson, and told him, you're too foul, your lies have caught up with you, you have a credibility gap going. This is in the American tradition: euphemisms to conceal the hard reality. They mean that he's a liar; that he's issued lying reports; that you can no longer believe in the statistics and the reports put out by his cabinet officers; that in fact, this country has been fed lies throughout its history. Lies on top of lies. Lies that dwindled into confusion and then more lies built out of the splinters of lies that had been shattered by reality. So that now we're faced with the situation where we have people in the black community tired of the lies, tired of the liars, and tired of the gradual and non-solutions. Not just Huey P. Newton, not just the members of the Black Panther Party, but black people throughout this country have turned away from the bootlicking leadership that we've been having for so long. They're turning to the streets, they're talking about Boston tea parties right here in Babylon, right here in California, in the streets of California. They're saying that we've had enough, that we will no longer take it; that you're threatening us with death, you're threatening us with genocide, so that we see no alternative but to organize ourselves to get into a position to take white people with us if we have to go. We say if there's going to be massive death for black people, the best that we can do is get into a position so that there'll be massive death for white people. Let's get into a position, inhabiting the cities as we do, inhabiting the core of the industrial system; let us get into a position so that if our enemies move against us to destroy us—and destruction does loom ominously on the horizon for us, we see that—let us be in a position to lay waste. Let us be in a position to disrupt the economic system, so that the military machine cannot function, so that the enemies of America can come in here and pick the gold out of the teeth of the Babylonians. And let us be in a position where we can say that if there's any victory over us, it will have to be a Pyrrhic victory, because we ain't going for it, because we recognize that the world situation today puts us in a position where we don't have to go for it.

We are not nihilists. We don't want to see destruction, so then we have to have an alternative. We're talking these days about an alternative, perhaps the last alternative, the last go-round. We go back to basic principles and we say that in order for this situation to be salvaged, we need sane people in this country; we need sane black people, and we need sane white people. Because we recognize that the Black Panther Party can't do it by itself, black people can't do it by themselves. It's going to take white people who recognize the situation that exists in this world today to stand up, yes, to unite with their black brothers and sisters. We're dealing with a situation where people have become antagonistic to each other, they've become estranged from each other, they've become hostile toward each other, and they've painted themselves into their various corners. And we say that this is exactly where the pigs of the power structure want to keep us.

Because it's still true that divide and conquer is the only sure way that tyrants, despots and racist pigs can insure victory over the people. We say that it's necessary to break out of those bags, to take steps, to create room for people to unite together; not on the basis of some phony, bleeding-heart liberalism; not on the basis of your looking at me and saying, Good luck, we hope that you win, we're watching you, and like someone said on the way in, "Courage!" Okay, we have to have courage, we have to have all of those things, but we also have to have help from people doing their job, doing your job.

A lot of people play the numbers game. They say, well, we have hydrogen bombs, we have the means to deliver those bombs, we have more guns than anyone in history's ever had—who can be a threat to us? There are a lot of people who are willing to stake the future of the entire planet on that. But there are other people on this earth who have guns, and there are other people on this earth who have hydrogen bombs, and they're taking the position that you push your button, they're going to push theirs. We say that's a just position, and our hang-up is that we recognize that we don't have time to produce scientists who then can go into laboratories and produce hydrogen bombs. Our position is that if we're going to have those bombs, we're going to have to take them from you. From the Babylonians. And they're here. And we have troops here. And we have a desperate feeling. We recognize that we must be in a position, if the guns and the bombs are going to be turned against us, to get our fingers on those bombs, so that if you drop it on me, I'm going to drop it on you. From now on, it's going to be democratic. We're going to have some democratic life, and we're going to have some democratic death. And there can't be no other way about that. No matter what you think about it, see? I know that people don't want to hear that. People want to hear people saying that everything is all right, that it's going to be all right, that things is getting better.

But we recognize that things are getting worse. Racist George Wallace is number two in the polls that they tell us about for President. And here we have a situation where the man who sends letters to black boys in the ghetto, sending them to Vietnam, General Hershey, is standing up saying that his choice for President is George Wallace. That's a desperate situation for black people, whether white people know it or not. It's a desperate situation for white people, because the world is on the brink, and it's rocking, idiots are rocking the boat. I'm one of those idiots, they say.

Ronald Reagan said that I'm rocking the boat, and I should be placed in a situation where I can no longer do that. Well, I'm going to rock it as long as I can. I feel that that's necessary—that when they threaten you, and tell you that you can't speak out, that you had better shut up or they'll revoke your parole, then it's necessary. I know that my parole officer has his representatives here. And for him, for Reagan, it's the same thing—baby, fuck you, because I'm going to say what I want to say. You can revoke my parole. It's not a question of playing games, it's not a question of making grandstand plays. It's a question of dealing with the situation the only way that it can be dealt with successfully, and that is to oppose, to resist.

I'm faced with the very real possibility of going back to prison, that's what they want me to do. I rule that out. I feel that when a man goes out to commit a crime, he has in his mind the possibility of getting caught, and he gets ready for the consequences. I know that I did that, when I used to go out and vamp on people, and do my thing. I knew what the penalty for that was, and I would say, if you play you have to pay. I did a little playing and I did a little paying, and I don't want to relate to that any more. But when some fool comes to me and tells me that he's going to send me back to prison because of the things that I say, later for him, later for his prisons, later for his momma. I'm not going to relate to that. I'm going to get together with people who can't relate to that, so that we can build the type of defensive mechanism that can offer a man some protection when he's confronted by pigs who want to keep him quiet, who want to confine him and put him in a little bitty cell.

I'm not thinking about myself, I'm thinking about Huey P. Newton, the Minister of Defense of the Black Panther Party, who has been railroaded through the courts of Oakland, by Judge Monroe Friedman, principally. I'm going to mention the fact that this is the eve of the Day of Atonement, isn't it? Judge Monroe Friedman is Jewish, isn't he? He had relatives who perished in the Warsaw ghetto. Tomorrow he will go to his synagogue to commemorate that, to commemorate his fellow Jews who perished and to think about those who presided over the final solution to the Jewish problem. And here he is with his funky ass, sitting on a bench, disgracing the very name of justice, presiding over the final solution to the Negro problem here in Babylon. Contradictions upon contradictions. Judge Monroe Friedman will be met tomorrow by a delegation of young Jewish people along with members of the Black

Panther Party. They will go to his synagogue to remind him and his fellow Jews of what he is getting into. We want his congregation to consider how they relate to this, and what they are going to do about it. It's their duty, just like it's your duty, because you may go to a church where my parole officer, or some prosecuting attorney, or some murderous, brutal policeman, sits side by side with you and looks up to Jesus and prays every Sunday with you. They don't go to the church that I would go to, if I related to that. They don't come into the black community to pray. They go into the white suburbs, they come down to Palo Alto, to Atherton, and to all of these places where they have a sanctuary. They go to all the places where the black community is kept out.

We're dealing with dissembling, now, with the walls of the ghetto. We're dealing with community imperialism. The black community is ruled by racist, exploiting elements who live in the white community: a coalition of white, avaricious businessmen, politicians, who are backed up by the gestapo police departments. They've turned the black community into a market: not any longer for cheap labor so much, but a market where they take welfare checks, they take the loot that we can steal and rob from the affluent white people in this country, and they suck it back through profits, and they leave us there. On top of us, we have a very vicious black bourgeoisie.

Confronted with this situation we have prayed in, we have crawled in, we have knelt in, everything, we have died in. They have passed laws, law on top of law, and we have George Wallace running for President. We have Lyndon Johnson in there now. Hubert Horatio Humphrey is laying to get into that. Richard Milhous Nixon looks like he's got it sewed up, and George Wallace is going to get in there if they mess up.

So what do we do? Sing "We Shall Overcome"? Tuck our tails and run when Reagan says that we can't go up to the campus to talk to the only sane people left in this society? No. Do we toss our guns into the churches and into the fire departments, as Mayor Joseph Alioto suggests? At the same time that they're escalating the armaments of the police departments? When Detroit was burning, when the freedom fighters there let themselves be heard, when they made manifest how they felt about this and when they set torches to the buildings and to whatever businesses they could get to, the city fathers didn't turn it over to the Department of Health, Education and Welfare, they turned it over to the Pentagon, to Robert Strange McNamara— the same man who then was presiding over the war in Vietnam.

We know how this society feels about us. We know that it has put us through all these changes. This society kidnapped us, brought us here and placed us in slavery. After that we were separate but equal; and now whatever this is, however you want to define it. But it's not freedom. It's not freedom, and we're still brutalized. Just the other day, a young black brother was shot to death by members of the Tactical Squad in San Francisco. People complain about the Tactical Squad. They called for a community review board for the police department, and the politicians, chambers of commerce, professional people, and white racists opposed that and said, We don't need that. What they're saying to us is, Let the niggers die. So where is our review board? There's going to be a review board or we're going to have to review it all in the streets.

Now, how do you analyze the situation when the Governor of the State of California freaks out when he finds that Eldridge Cleaver has been invited to participate in an experimental course? He runs down to Los Angeles, grabs the week-kneed Regents by the scruffs of their necks, and places his political pressure on them, forcing them to say that Eldridge Cleaver cannot deliver ten lectures, only one. My response to that, the response of the students at Cal, and the response of the faculty members who sponsored the whole thing, is: not only will I deliver the ten, I'm going to deliver twenty, and later for Mickey Mouse, and later for Donald Duck.

It is necessary to remind certain people in this country that it doesn't belong to the pigs of the power structure, that Ronald Reagan doesn't own the people of the State of California, he doesn't own the government of the State of California. In fact he is a public servant become arrogant, like all public servants these days. They insult you when you go to talk to them about some need or some service they're supposed to perform. They're all out of order, from the police to the clerks in the buildings downtown; all of them act as though they own it, when in fact you pay their salary with your taxes, and if anybody belongs to anybody, they belong to the people. They're treating us as though we belonged to them. They have usurped the machinery of government in this country; they call it representative democracy, but it represents nothing but the pigs of the power structure.

We're living in a situation where professional police departments in this country have developed a caste consciousness. They have all the attributes of motivation that you have in the military service. They see themselves as guarding the frontiers of a civilization against barbarian hordes. And we're the barbarian hordes. The people are the barbarian hordes. If you stand up and demand to be heard, if you say that you're going to exercise your Constitutional right and state your position on the war in Vietnam, and the police are given orders by the plain-clothes pigs, they'll come down and shoot mace in your face. Or they will shoot you and they will kill you. They will follow out their orders and tell you later on, or tell your survivors, as Adolf Eichmann told the people, that they were just doing their duty. But we say that the duty of a policeman is to shoot his superior officer when he orders him to turn his guns and his clubs and his mace against the people. That's his duty: to arrest him if not shoot him. If you can't relate to shooting him, at least arrest him. If you don't want him arrested, at least come outside, hold a press conference, tell us about it.

I know there must be some pigs within that pig pen that don't go along with that shit. Or are they all insane? Are they that uptight together? Does every policeman on the Oakland Police Department go along with the insane activity of two drunken pigs who drive by the office of the Black Panther Party and shoot it up like a shooting gallery? Does every officer on that force go along with that? We haven't seen any evidence of them coming out and denouncing that. We haven't seen any evidence of them resigning in protest over that. What we did see was two hundred of them threatening not to come to work next day if the two officers were disciplined. That's what they did. Threatened to go on strike. These two—but it wasn't even two, there were six of them—were identified because they were riding in a marked car. They had on their uniforms, the car had numbers on the side, and some citizen wrote down the numbers and turned it in. That blew their game, you see? But the others, the others in those plain cars, they got away. Lying Chief Gaines knows that they were there. He knows it. But he came out and told the people, well, don't condemn the whole barrel because there are two rotten apples in it. And we know that he was lying when he said that, and he knew he was lying. The Oakland Police Department—I'm going to just say it—like all police departments in this country, is rotten from top to bottom and it's got to be put in order by the people. We cannot allow them to pass and enforce all this legislation that will give them increased arms while they disarm the people, seeing how they treat the people. And are we going to sit back and be smug and silent? Are we going to observe that and say, Well, niggers going to have a hard time next summer? It's not going to be just the niggers. It's going to be white niggers. White, simple-minded people, Babylonians, devoid of any ability to reason through what's going on in this world. College students are perhaps the only people left who can deal with this. That is why we were very glad when we were invited to go down to that campus and talk to the young white people there; because they're the ones who are outraged by this.

I have a thing with these old people. I'm old myself, you dig? I'm no young chicken. I'm thirty-three years old. At that age, I'm one of the oldest people in the Black Panthers. Up until recently, I felt very much alone.

Before I was married—my wife is in the audience—
there was one pretty little girl. I said, "Say, why don't
you go with me tonight?" She said, "Oh, Eldridge,
you're like a father to me." So if I'm going to be like
a father to her, then I'm going to be like a father to
you. I'm going to be like a father to all you old people
there, I'm going to be like a father to all the pigs of
the mass media who come to meetings, listen to what
you say, and then go back and write their lies like some
jackass from *Newsweek* who came down to the Barristers' Club in San Francisco and sat there with his
tape recorder. He listened very intently and then went
back and wrote something that seemed like a nightmare he'd had that night, and, like he wrote down his
nightmare, because it didn't relate to anything that we
had to say.

What we had to say then is generally what we say
right now. And we take very great pains to leave a loophole for those white people who want to get through
there. We know that people don't like to be condemned
categorically, and we don't like to make our condem-
nations categorical. We want to leave a loophole for
those who recognize the situation we're confronted with
today, who recognize that the world has become a death
row for everybody, and who want to see a future for
the people; who want to see a future for everybody,
not just themselves, and who want to see a future where
there's freedom; who want to see a future where there's
justice, who want to see a future where there's no more
restraint upon people by others who exploit them and
grow fat while the exploited grow skinny from a lack
of all the things that a good society must have. We
start with the basic principle that every man, woman

and child on the face of the earth deserves the very highest standard of living that human knowledge and technology is capable of providing. Period. No more than that, no less than that. Anything that stands in the way of that principle is a contradiction in terms of the survival of people. It's evil and it has to be removed.

Looking around today, we find ourselves in the pretty position of having to say that America the beautiful, unmasked as America the ugly, America the hideous, America the horrible, the torturer and the murderer of mankind, has become successor to Nazi Germany. America is, in fact, the number one obstacle to human progress on the face of the earth today. Not Russia, not China, but Babylon, right here in North America, that's right here. That's right here, a country erected on the bones of the red man, a country erected on the graves and with the sweat of black men and women; a country erected upon the backs of white people; a country erected at the expense of humanity; a country created out of exploitation, avaricious land-grabbing, murder, genocide—called manifest destiny. Manifest destiny. So we're living in the time of the last go-round, where there's going to be peace and freedom or there's going to be chaos, confusion, and death.

Good white people, you've got to support me, George Wallace, you've got to support me, Law and Order Nixon, you've got to support me, Meathead Me-too Humphrey, you've got to support me—or else the niggers are going to come into the white suburbs and turn the white suburbs into shooting galleries. And I'm not here campaigning for your vote. Because I wouldn't give a damn if you didn't go to the polls in November. As a matter of fact, if you're going to vote for one of those pigs, I would strongly recommend that you didn't go. You see, if you vote for Richard Nixon, if you vote for Meathead Humphrey, if you vote for George Wallace, you are voting for a continuation and an escalation of the policies and the pretenses that have brought the world to the brink of disaster. Nixon would want to attack China. Humphrey would do it. George Wallace would attack everybody.

And just to show you how propaganda is used and how people are manipulated, take a look at George Wallace. You know that he's a racist pig, that he lacks style, and that he doesn't represent a future, not even for the racists in this country, because everybody's hip to him. So here we see him putting his ugly face on the fronts of magazines, we see polls compiled by all the pigs, shot out into the pig media, telling you that Wallace has a boom going, he's number two in the polls. No motherfucker came to ME and asked me how I felt about George Wallace. They didn't ask me that. What they did was take some numbers and some lying men of words, pigs of the mass media, NBC, ABC, and so forth, and wrote that shit, and put it out; and now people are going around saying, yeah, Wallace got a thing going. But that's Republican money, I would say, put out by Richard Milhous Nixon to establish an extreme opposite to himself or to his right. Then he can say, well, Wallace is on the right, Humphrey's on the left, and here I am in the middle. But when you look at that and when you see him, and he says those things like, "I'll debate Humphrey but I won't debate Wallace," the only thing I can see him say is Oink. And that's all. Because he's lying, he's playing a trick bag, and the people, like sheep, are jumping into it. There are some people in this country who one day oppose Wallace because they have been programmed to oppose him, who are now reprogrammed and now they say well, he's got a boom going for him so I'm going to vote for Wallace, because he represents dissent. You see. He comes out and says that we've got to do away with federal government and we don't have anything left but federal government.

There aren't any more state governments. We have these honorary pigs like Mayor Alioto or whoever your mayor might be here, presiding over the distribution of a lot of federal funds. He's plugged into one gigantic system, one octopus spanning the continent from one end to the other, reaching its tentacles all around the world, in everybody's pocket and around everybody's neck. We just have one octopus. A beast with his head wherever LBJ might be tonight. That's all we have: one monstrosity that has to be dealt with on the local level, on the state level, on the national level, on the international level. So we have to relate to our allies locally, we have to relate to our allies on the state level, nationally and internationally. Internationally we have to place ourselves in the Third World, with the oppressed people of the world against the pigs, the international pig power structure.

We have to have solidarity starting with the most extreme enemy that they pose for you, the People's Republic of China, Mao Tse-tung, baby, you've done a beautiful job. You've got your hydrogen bombs, you don't have your troops on anyone else's soil, you're there defending your own borders, and if they attack you, drop your bomb, bomb right here on my head. Blow me up and take these Babylonians with me. Let the people of the world have some peace. We want solidarity with Ho Chi Minh, solidarity with the people, the Viet Cong, the Liberation fighters in Vietnam.

I'm sorry for our boys. Let's support our boys. Let's bring them home, let's don't put them on the police forces when we bring them home. Let's get them out of there just as quick as we possibly can get the boats over there and get them out. But when we get them back, let's not put them on the police departments like they want to do. Let's tell them that if they want to defend the people, they can form a people's militia, and defend the people against these usurpers, against these pigs in the local police department who have grown so arrogant as to turn their murderous weapons against the people.

We need protection from the pigs. If you can't relate to that, then you're with the pigs, you're endorsing the pigs, whether you know it or not, whether you want to or not. Because it's been said that today, you're part of the solution or you're part of the problem. There is no more middle ground, because the problem is rampant, the problem is a problem of survival, of blood, of your heart beating, of the hearts of people continuing to beat.

You're faced with that, as the people in Nazi Germany were faced with it, and you can puzzle and you can equivocate and you can sit there and tell me that you don't know whether you want to support black people of the pigs. You can say: I see you there getting your head beat, I see you there getting shot to death, but I don't know if I'm going to help you or not. How can the hostility help but become general?

How can I not be hostile toward people who take

a neutral position while these militant racists are vamping on me and killing me and depriving me and loved ones of life, liberty and the pursuit of happiness? How can I not feel some hostility toward you when you raise your Declaration of Independence, when you raise your Constitution and your Bill of Rights, and you point to the freedom that's recorded there in words, and tell me by your actions that it's not for me, or that you don't give a damn whether I have it or not?

And some very interesting laws are being passed. They don't name me; they don't say, take the guns away from the niggers. They say that the people no longer will be allowed to have that. They don't pass these rules and these regulations specifically for black people, they have to pass them in a way that will take in everybody. Hubert Humphrey says it's the hippies, the yippies and the Panthers. Gestapo Chief J. Edgar Hoover says it's the SDS and the Panthers. What they're all saying is they have white people in this country who are dissenting, and they have some black people who are dissenting, and that these people are a threat to the game that's being run on people, and they have to be isolated, exterminated, confined to concentration camps, or have their paroles revoked, dig it? That's what they're saying.

Here, at rich, palatial Stanford University, you can assume that you are going to continue running around this campus, thinking that you're free, or assuming that you're free, and that you're going to be allowed to do that, because there may be two, three, four, maybe a boxcarful of white radicals on this campus. Maybe when my parole officer comes looking for me, to lock me up, I'll be hiding in the house of one of these white radicals. So that the pig is not going to just need a search warrant that will allow him to come and kick down my door, he's going to have to have a search warrant that will allow him to kick down everyone's door. And I'm glad, because I'm tired of having my door kicked down while other people have security and use it to say all right to oppression, and raise not a murmur against it. I say that if they kick down one door, let all the doors be kicked down! Let all the doors be kicked down, don't just kick my door down! I want them to kick your door down. One of the reasons that I came down here tonight, the reason that I'm willing to go to all of these campuses and talk is because it places you in a position of defying Mickey Mouse; because whether or not Stanford is tired of the University of California complex, it is still an educational institution, and by inviting me here you're telling Ronald Reagan, Fuck you, Ronald Reagan. And he has to be told that.

Every Ronald Reagan, every Max Rafferty, every George Wallace, every Richard Nixon, every Hubert Humphrey from one end of this country to the other, all around the world, wherever they might be found, must be told that, and not only do they have to be told, but we've got to start dragging them out of those offices by their ears, if we can't get them at the ballot box. If they have reached the ballot box in such a way that your candidate cannot even be placed for nomination at the convention, that you're hit in the mouth with a club when you try to speak his name, then they're forcing you to take it to the streets, with the niggers. The niggers have been waiting on you for four hundred years. And they're in a position where they can't really wait for you to come. They've got to move on, and create room, create conditions, so that the pigs of the power structure will be forced to become more and more repressive in order to continue their exploitation.

I want to apologize right here. I want to apologize to Ronald Reagan. Because I've said that he's been responsible for a lot of the things that he does. And the poor boy's not. He's not responsible. What he has is the type of memory, you could put a script before him, and whether it's Wild Bill Hickock or Mickey Mouse, he can play the role to a grade-B level. I mean, he can't really get into a smooth thing, he's grade-B; I might be giving him too much, you see. But it's the script-writers who write his scripts for him. Who writes Max Rafferty's scripts? It's just possible that, being a political beggar as he is, he might write his own scripts. They sound like that, quack, quack, quack.

Someone said tonight that Max Rafferty has a Ph.D. in physical education, in football and baseball and basketball and ball-head, I don't know. I don't know what his credentials are. I know that he has a yackety-yak mouth and I can only relate to one adversary at a time. I want to challenge Max Rafferty to a duel, but he's obviously too old to whip me, I could kick his ass. But I challenged Ronald Reagan to a duel, and I reiterate that challenge tonight. I say that Ronald Reagan is a punk, a sissy and a coward, and I challenge him to a duel, I challenge him. I challenge him to a duel to the death or until he says Uncle Eldridge. And I give him his choice of weapons. He can use a gun, a knife, a baseball bat or a marshmallow. And I'll beat him to death with a marshmallow. That's how I feel about him. Here is a man, a demagogue, in the negative sense. I'm a demagogue—in the positive sense. But here, here is a negative demagogue. He is willing to corrupt any process in order to capitalize on their corruption for one ballot box in November. Here's a man, Max Rafferty, Superintendent of Public Instruction, who is willing to destroy academic freedom so that he can get his idiotic ass into the Senate—with the other idiots that are there. He wants to be our second Senator, second to the song and dance man, Murphy.

They say that people get the rulers that they deserve. I'll be damned if I deserve Ronald Reagan. I definitely don't deserve Max Rafferty; none of us deserves Richard Nixon. Do we deserve a mealy-mouthed vacillating coward like Hubert Humphrey? And do we deserve George Wallace? Well, you got them. Now what're you going to do about that? You have pigs, who are pissed on the Constitution, and throw it in the faces of people and say that they are going to run this thing the way they want to, whether you like it or not.

There can be no adequate response to that except the revolutionary movement that can unite the people who have been ruled out. Unite them, and arm them with every revolutionary tool in history, from pencil and paper to the gun. Our adversaries have everything from pencil and paper to the gun, and beyond the gun to hydrogen bombs; we have to face that. We either have to put our heads underground and avoid it, or we have to do something about it.

Now, Huey P. Newton says that the spirit of the people is greater than the Man's technology. It's a lie when they say that the people no longer have spirit. I would even go so far as to say that it's not true that the American people are evil and corrupt as a whole.

I have never believed it, and I don't believe it now. What I do believe is that the American people have been brainwashed, they've brainwashed themselves. It has got so confused that brainwashers themselves brainwash—graduate from these institutions and proceed to brainwash future generations.

Someone asked me earlier tonight if I thought that the Europeans, when they came here from Europe, had a racist program for the world. And looking at history you see that that was truly not the case. You have some poverty-stricken people that were hungry, on a desolate piece of earth, getting into ships, going around the world, looking at the way other people were doing things. You remember Marco Polo? Well, Marco Polo didn't drive into China in a Cadillac. Marco Polo came into China raggedy and damn near dead, and the Chinese laid him out on a piece of silk and nursed him back to life. The Pilgrims, the founding fathers of Babylon, didn't sail here on the *Queen Mary*. They came here damned near dead, fell onto Plymouth Rock and the Indians taught them how to survive. They taught them turkey, they taught them fishing, they taught them corn. I remember a book that I had in grammar school. The title of a chapter—and Rafferty probably burnt this book up already—was, "The First Five Years Were the Hardest." They talked about the trials and tribulations of those who landed in Jamestown, Virginia, and Plymouth Rock, and all that jazz. How they suffered during the cold winters, how they suffered through the summers, and how they just suffered for five years. They could not have survived if the Indians hadn't given them the benefit of their technology.

But there had been a lot of history that had gone down by that time. There had been wars in Europe for hundreds of years by then. Marco Polo had long been in his grave. Alexander the Great had been snooping around the world. Caravans of Europeans combed the earth and saw the riches of other lands, they saw other people with other ways of life. They saw gunpowder in China, and they saw ways of putting that together to making a boomstick that could defeat a spear, a bow and arrow. They saw that they could take all this land, they could colonize the world. They could take Africa, Asia and Latin America—The New World, and make it into their image, like the Old World. And make slavery universal. They saw that they could do this. And they competed with each other to see who would do it. And they defeated each other, and they warred against each other.

They kidnapped black people from Africa and brought them over here, and called that slavery. Called us Negroes and now they call us free. This whole world situation was created by that process. When the Christians, or those that say they are Christians, found themselves locked in certain ideological ambiguities, they said, "What are these people, are they human souls also? If they're human souls then they could be Christians too. And if they could be Christians, how could we justify exploiting them?"

The Pope went into his chamber, with the other pigs. Because they have been pigs to black people too, they have been pigs to the oppressed. The religious leaders that sprinkle holy water on hydrogen bombs; who go to Vietnam and bless the boys; who prayed for victory, for policies of LBJ. What are they, if they're not pigs of

the cloth? And I don't care if they say a eulogy over me
or not. They can spit on me and flush me down the
toilet when I'm gone. I don't need their holy water,
I don't need their prayers. How can I relate to that
when they are sanctifying oppression? And the oppressors have no rights that the oppressed are bound
to respect. I can respect them when they throw down
their turned around collars, and get out in the streets
with the people, hold their Bible in one hand and a
gun in the other and say, freedom for the people—
give us Liberty, or we're going to give you death.

That goes for everybody. They said that I advocated
fighting lawyers. Lawyers that would go into those
courtrooms and deal with tyrants, foul thieves like
Judge Monroe Friedman. Deal with him with the law
book and if he refuses to relate to that, deal with him
with a gun. For Monroe Friedman and all the other
pigs on the bench. They are condemning the Bible,
Isaiah and Samuel, I'm getting some references here
because I'm going to have to defend this, in my next
life. But I'm going to say the same thing then, and
I'll defend that one in my next one because had they
not been judged and condemned throughout history?
Is there not evidence, testimony on record to show that
there were Pharisees and Sadducees, blocking the way
to salvation for the people?

When we look at other countries, we can see the
rulers of other countries, acting in a very undesirable
manner. We can see people in other countries being
railroaded. But when we've come right here in Babylon
and looked at what's going on right here, we say . . .
well, you win some, you lose some. We can look at
Martin Luther King, and turn him into a thing, for-

getting completely that Martin Luther King had a longer arrest record than I do. Martin Luther King had a string of arrests as long as my arm, but they arrested Martin Luther King the same way that they arrested members of the Black Panther Party, for the very same things, standing up and telling it like it is. That's what he was doing, Martin Luther King was running it down. He was leading people out into the streets, nonviolently, peacefully, and he offered up his life as a sacrifice, and the racists took it. And they took nonviolence with them. The bullet that killed Martin Luther King murdered nonviolence, and left the bullet and the echo of the bullet here in Babylon for us to deal with. And we might be wrong. Martin Luther King just might be right.

Maybe everything we're doing is wrong, because we don't know about the universe. I don't know whether there's an old man up there with a beard. I don't know if I'm going to be thrown before his throne and sentenced to hellfire and brimstone and damnation throughout eternity. But I know one thing, that I can't relate to that either. Because if he casts me down into the hellfire, I'm going to look around for you. I'm going to look around for the members of the Black Panther Party, and say, brothers, let's get this shit together and deal with the devil. Because we cannot relate to this. I think that could possibly be classified as oppression on a celestial scale. And if God forms a coalition with the devil to keep us there we're going to have to deal with him. Because the spirit of the people would be greater than that technology.

The point is, that you don't have to accept it. There are more people in this country than there are pigs. They can bluff us and they can frighten us, but united they cannot defeat us. We could corral them, we could re-tire them, and we could run down a program on them that would put them in their place, and we have to start doing that now. The key note of the Black Panther Party's program in this time, is for the decentralization of the institutions of this society. We want to decentral-ize the police department. We want to decentralize the educational institutions, because we need a Stanford for black people. We need a Stanford for black people be-cause black people cannot relate to education that teaches them that they are inferior, and that the white people are superior, and that it's going to be that way forever because that's the way that God made it. We say let white people have their educational institutions. We say that white people should have their educational in-stitutions and let them go in there and get themselves together and give themselves an education. And we will be more than glad to participate in that, ten lectures or twenty lectures, or just one on the run, or none, what-ever we can do to help that.

And we would want to recognize that we need insti-tutions that can give us the education that's necessary to cope with our environment. Recognize that this de-cadent system is part of our environment. Racism is the rattlesnake in our environment. Education is supposed to teach you to cope with your environment. To deal with the problem of your environment. We need an education that will teach us to cope with white suprem-acy, white racism, and with the murderous institutions of this society. We would want you to endorse that, to help us do that, to participate in that. And to give what-ever you can, if it means to give instruction, if it means to build the buildings. We feel that it's necessary to create situations where people can relate to each other, unite with each other and defend each other against all of the evils that threaten everybody. And that's not an obnoxious goal. It's only obnoxious to those who cling so much to an ideology called integration that in order to hold onto it they are willing to gloss over all the problems remaining. But we say that we are going to have to do some disentangling, because what integration amounts to is decentralized segregation. That's all it is.

Decentralized segregation. We walk and talk among you, and we're colonial subjects right here in Babylon. We're colonial subjects in a decentralized colony, dispersed throughout the white mother country in enclaves called black communities, black ghettos. But this is a process that started with the colonialism that spread around the world. Now forces are moving for liberation in these other colonies around the world; the same spirit motivates the Vietnamese people to pick up a gun and run the Yankees, the French, the Japanese and everybody else out of there that comes in there to oppress them and exploit them. That same human spirit, which is universal, also today motivates black people right here among you in Babylon, in these black ghettos. And we've got to have it. We've got to have liberation. Part of that liberation is the process of decentralizing the colony. Breaking down the walls of the colony, and moving for liberation. People ask us, how do you feel about integration, how do you feel about separation?

The position of the Black Panther Party is that in the past there have been too many people, too many splinter organizations coming along—"We speak for all black people, we want to be integrated;" "We speak for all black people and we want to be separated." We say that there's no organization; no man in history has ever had a mandate from black people on that particular issue, on separation or integration. And so we feel that the only way that it can be decided is through a democratic process, not through some of these rigged polls. The question has to be decided by a United Nations supervised plebiscite. Machinery should be set up throughout this country that will allow black people to go into a voting booth and cast a ballot, stating whether or not they want to be integrated or whether or not they want to be separated, and have this land partitioned, so that they can build a nation of their own, or do they want to be part of the American stew here in the Babylonian melting pot? I think that's their decision. I think it's very clear that all people have a right to go on record about their destiny. And I don't think there's anyone who has the right to stand up and say, well, no you can't have that.

As a matter of fact, I would favor two plebiscites. I would like to have a plebiscite that will allow white people to go on record and let us know once and for all: do you want to be in a nation where black people are part of the citizenry, or do you want to be separated into your own white country? I think we need two plebiscites in this country, so that we will know whether or not to get behind George Wallace and Elijah Muhammad, to get behind the many others who speak of many other alternatives. We need to know that; it has to become part of the record. Once we have that information, we can move on to solve the problem, because our direction will be clear, our tactics will flow from that decision. The Black Panther Party takes that position.

People ask us if we are racists. We don't like to respond to that any more. We say, go ask the white members of the white Peace and Freedom Party. They might tell you today that Eldridge Cleaver is a dictator or something, in terms of how he moves, on the presidential thing. They might say bad things, individually, about individual members of the Black Panther Party. But they will not say that Eldridge Cleaver or the Black Panther Party is a racist organization. We feel that it is necessary to get those things out of the way because the mass media, the people who put out propaganda, like for it to be said so that people can get confused and react to that. Even in the black community if you tag a man as being a racist, if you tag an organization as being racist, a lot of black people get uptight about it. They won't relate to that. For all these hundreds of years black people have had the thrust of their hearts against racism, because racism has been what has been murdering them. So black people oppose racism. The Black Panther Party opposes it, and we would hope that everybody can oppose it whether it's black or white. Because it will do us no good. It will only get us killed, and it will destroy the world.

I don't know if what I said here tonight has been worth your wait. I hope that I haven't just totally disappointed you. But I have one more thing to say and it's not to all you ugly men in the audience. This is for the ladies. I want to say to the ladies, and I remind you that we're not playing any games, that a very serious situation exists. You have the power to bring a squeaking halt to a lot of things that are going on, and we call that pussy power. We say that political power, revolutionary power grows out of the lips of a pussy. I'm sorry for all the Victorians who have had their morals ruffled, but just sit still for a minute and you'll come back to earth. Cool it, see. We have said that you're either part of the solution, or you're part of the problem. If you're part of the solution, what do you look like laying up with part of the problem? Everything can be progressive, everything can be revolutionary. Love can be progressive, sex can be revolutionary. And it can be counterrevolutionary, it can be reactionary, or conservative, if you lay up with Mickey Mouse or Donald Duck. I want to make a point. You look at these males who call themselves men, and tell them that they're going to have to become part of the solution or don't call you up on the telephone any more. Don't write you love letters, and don't come around knocking on your door. Tell them to go away, listen to some of Bobby Dylan's records, or something. Tell them to get themselves together, and then come back. And you can do that. You can put them under more pressure than I can with speeches. You can cut off their sugar. And you can have them all running around here acting like Lenin, Mao Tse-tung and Jerry Rubin. And if you don't believe it, just try it. Put them up tight. And if they don't want to act right, I'm sure that there are a lot of people who'd be willing to put their phone numbers on the bulletin boards out there who will come to your aid in your hour of need. Thank you.

I want to say "all power to the people. Black power to black people, white power to white people." And do you get uptight about that, because you haven't had white people, you've had pig power? You haven't had any white power. We say, power to the people, all people should have the power to control their own destiny. White people should have the power to control their own destiny. Eskimos and Indians, every living ass and swinging dick. Everyone should have the power to control that destiny. And you have had history, you've had government of the pigs, by the pigs and for the pigs. You've had history written by pigs, to edify pigs and to brutalize our minds. We say that we have to close the book on history today, close the book on everything, everything up to today. We date it from March the 15th of this year, when the Black Panther Party formed a coalition with the Peace and Freedom Party. At that point, at the Richmond Auditorium, we closed the book on American history, stamped it with a pig hoof, and said that's pig history.

Let's put it in the museums and open a new book and let the people write a history fit to be taught to their children: a history that we can all look to, and agree that that is the truth, that we won't have to be ashamed of it. Let's agree that we won't have to duplicate our institutions of learning so that we can be sure we will get an education that will enable us to cope with our environment, because what we need in fact today, and what we're really lagging behind in, are necessities. We need a university of the world that can teach the whole world—all the people of the world—the true history of the world; not a racist history, not a nationalist history, but a history that can enable people to live. And we need a society that will be universal, with no passports, no boundaries, a utopia brought down to earth, a classless society, a society that is not based on capitalistic economics and exploitation. Yes.

Let's pay our respects to Brother Karl Marx's gigantic brain, using the fruits of his wisdom, applying them to this crumbling system, and have some socialism, moving on to the classless society. You call it communism. If you get uptight about that, we can redefine that; we don't have to quibble over words, and we can call it a human society. It's not going to be the Great Society, because that stinks. It's not going to be Richard Milhous Nixon's society—he's not going to be here 'cause he has to go. All of his ilk, all of the pigs of the power structure, all have to be barbecued or they have to change their way of living. We have to get into a society that can comprehend the world, that can deal with the distribution of labor and distribution of production on a world-wide level. Then we will have a basis for really looking up into the stars and coping with the rest of our environment beyond this very narrow planet.

Dealing with ourselves, dealing with the social scientists—the social sciences, excuse me—we can become human, we can change this barbaric, Babylonian, decadent, racist monstrosity into a civilization, and we can help the world by helping ourselves right here. If we give freedom to ourselves right in Babylon, we will give freedom to the world, and we can then take these guns and have some disarmament, we can have some gun control, and you will be able to walk down your streets at night without worrying about somebody like me or some other crazy nigger or a Mexican or another crazy hippie or a Yippie leaping out on you to get some funds or whatever else you have that he might want.

I know that I don't feel good paying taxes because I recognize that the tax system in this country is nothing but a fund-raising device for the pigs of the power structure and I don't relate to paying for my own destruction. I said that I was going to give my taxes to Joan Baez, and tell her to do what she wants, I don't care. But my wife corrected me and said to me, "No, don't do that, give it to the Huey P. Newton Defense Fund," and that makes sense, so I'm going to do that. I'm going to write that check, I'm going to sign it myself, and later for J. Edgar Hoover, later for his mammy, later for the Secret Service, later for all of that because we have to get into a situation where the madmen come forth.

When the sane people don't do it, when all the good middle class people don't do it, then the madmen have to do it, and the madmen say that we're going to have freedom or we're going to have chaos; we're going to be part of the total destruction of America or we're going to be part of the liberation of America. And if you kill me, well I'll just lay me down to rest, you dig it, and all power to the people. I'm very glad to have been here, and in closing, I'll repeat, Down with the pigs of the power structure. Back to Disneyland for Mickey Mouse. Thank you.

October 1, 1968

FAREWELL ADDRESS

The California Appeals Court overruled Judge Sherwin's writ of habeas corpus, and Eldridge Clever was scheduled to surrender to the prison authorities on November 27, 1968. Five days before his surrender date Cleaver spoke at a San Francisco meeting on behalf of his defense. As it worked out, this was his last public appearance before he became a "fugitive" from California, and then federal, law.

Good evening, everybody. Kind of stuck for words tonight. I don't know whether this is a hello or a goodbye. I talked to my parole officer today, and he told me that on Wednesday the 27th he wanted me to call him up about 8:30 in the morning, so he could tell me where to meet him so he could transport me to San Quentin. They want to have a parole revocation hearing, and I guess they think they have a right to do that. They certainly are proceeding as though they have a right. Having had some experience with them, I know that when they have you in their clutches, they proceed with what they want to do whether they have a right or not.

A lot of people don't know anything about the prison system. I think they make the same mistake looking at prison officials as they do with cops: they think that in some sense they are guardians of the law; that they're there to protect society, and everything they say is the truth; that there's nothing wrong with what they're into, and nothing wrong with what they're doing. Well, I know. Not so much in my own case, but from the cases of others that I've observed in the various prisons in the State of California. There are a whole lot of people behind those walls who don't belong there. And everybody behind those walls is being subjected to programs that are not authorized, nor related to the reasons for which they were sent there.

Rehabilitation in the State of California is less than a bad joke. I don't even know how to relate to that word, "rehabilitation." It presupposes that at one time one was "habilitated," and that somehow he got off the right track and was sent to this garage, or repair shop, to be dealt with and then released. Rehabilitated, and placed back on the right track. Well, I guess that the right track has to be this scene out here: the free world. Convicts call us out here the "free world." After you're behind those walls for a while, I guess it starts looking like the Garden of Eden. They can't see all of the little conflicts that are going on out here. Alioto [San Francisco Mayor Joseph Alioto] doesn't look as much like Al Capone from that distance. That's right. Al Capone, Alioto— Big Al. Alley-oop Oto. You know. People yearn, people *yearn*, behind those walls, to return to the free world. To return to society. To be free, and not to be returned to the penitentiary.

Now, when I went into the penitentiary I made a decision. I took a long hard look at myself and I said, well, you've been walking this trip for a little too long, you've tired of it. It's very clear that what you had going for yourself before you came in was not adequate. While you're here you're going to have to work with yourself, deal with yourself, so that when you get out of here you're going to stay out. Because it was pretty clear to me that that was my last go-round, that I could not relate to prison any more. So I guess I developed something of a social conscience. I decided to come out here and work with social problems, get involved with the Movement and make whatever contribution I possibly could. When I made that decision, I thought that the parole authorities would be tickled pink with me, because they were always telling me to do exactly that. They would tell me I was selfish. They would ask me why I didn't start relating to other people, and looking beyond the horizons of myself.

So I did that, you know. And I just want to tell you this. I've had more trouble out of parole officers and the Department of Corrections simply because I've been relating to the Movement than I had when I was committing robberies, rapes and other things that I didn't get caught for. That's the truth. If I was on the carpet for having committed a robbery, well, there would be a few people uptight about that. But it seemed to be localized. It didn't seem to affect the entire prison system or the entire parole board. They didn't seem to have much time to discuss it, you know. They run you through their meetings very, very briefly. You feel that your case is not even being considered. But I know that now my case is constantly on their desks, and my parole officer doesn't have very much to do except keep track of me. He wants to know where I go, how much money I make each month, where I'm living, when I'm going to go out of town, phone him up when I get back to town, and ask his permission to do this and that.

There's something more dangerous about attacking the pigs of the power structure verbally than there is in walking into the Bank of America with a gun and attacking it forthrightly. Bankers hate armed robbery, but someone who stands up and directly challenges their racist system, that drives them crazy. I don't know if there are any bankers in the audience tonight, but I hope that there are. I hope that there's at least one, or a friend of one, or somebody who will carry the message to one. And I hope particularly that there's one here from the Bank of America. I heard today on the news that brother Cesar Chavez has declared war on the Bank of America. The Bank of America is Alioto's bank. My wife told me this evening that she received a phone call from the Bank of America saying that they were going to repossess our car because we were three months behind in our payments. That's not true, but I wished that I had never paid a penny for it. I wished that I could have just walked onto that lot and said, "Stick 'em up, motherfucker! I'm taking this." Because that's how I felt about it. That's how I feel about it now. I don't relate to this system of credit—see it now, take it home, pay later . . . but make sure you pay.

It was only out of consideration for the atmosphere that I would need in order to do the other things I wanted to do that I didn't rip it off. Or that I haven't walked into the Bank of America. Or that I haven't walked into any other establishment and repossessed the loot that they have in there. So I don't know what they expect from me, see? I haven't committed any crimes. I don't feel there's a need for rehabilitation. I don't feel the need of going back to Dirty Red's penitentiary. Warden Nelson [Warden of San Quentin]? The prison guards call him Big Red, but the convicts call him Dirty Red. He's sitting over there across the bay and he's waiting for me, because we have a little history of friction. He doesn't like me. My parole officer doesn't like me. He tells the newspaper writers, "Yeah, I think he's a real nice fellow. I think he's made an excellent adjustment. If it wasn't for this particular indictment brought against him, I'd be perfectly willing to have him as my parolee from now on." Yet if you go down to the parole department and ask them to let you see my file, you will find just one charge against me, other than those lodged against me in Alameda County, which are yet to be adjudicated. I haven't gone to trial for those. I have pleaded "Not Guilty" to them. The one legitimate charge they have is "failing to cooperate with the parole agent."

The first time I saw that, I couldn't understand what it meant, because I bent over backwards to cooperate with that punk. So I asked him, "Just what does that mean? What's the substance of that?" Now this is going to really surprise you. He said, "Do you remember when you went to New York to tape the David Susskind Show?" I said, "Yes, I remember doing that."

"Remember I told you that when you got back you should give me a phone call and let me know you were back in town?"

"Yes, and I did that, didn't I?"

"No, you didn't do it. That's against the rules."

And that's the only thing that they have in my file that is even debatable. All the other things that they are hostile towards me for, they can't put in the files because it's against the law. It's contrary to the Constitution and they would be ashamed to write it down on paper and place it in my file. They probably have another file that they smuggle around between them. But they cannot come out and tell you one thing that I've done that would justify returning me to the penitentiary.

I just have to say that I didn't leave anything in that penitentiary except half of my mind and half of my soul, and that's dead there. I have no use for it. It's theirs. They can have that. That's my debt to them. That's my debt to society, and I don't owe them a motherfucking thing! They don't have anything coming. Everything they get from now on, they have to take! I believe that our time has come. A point has been reached where a line just has to be drawn, because the power structure of this country has been thoroughly exposed. There is no right on their side. We know that they're moving against people for political purposes.

There's a favorite line of mine. It says that there is a point where caution ends and cowardice begins. Everybody is scared of the pigs, of the power structure. The people have reason to be concerned about them because they have these gestapo forces that they issue orders to. They come in with their clubs and their guns, and they will exterminate you, if that's what it takes to carry out the will of their bosses.

I don't know how to go about waiting until people start practicing what they preach. I don't know how to go about waiting on that. Because all I see is a very critical situation, a chaotic situation where there's pain, there's suffering, there's death, and I see no justification for waiting until tomorrow to say what you could say tonight. I see no justification for waiting until other people get ready. I see no justification for not moving even if I have to move by myself. I think of my attitude towards these criminals—my parole officer included—who control the prison system, who control the parole board. I can't reconcile things with them because for so long I've watched them shove shit down people's throats. I knew there was something wrong with the way that they were treating people. I knew that by no stretch of the imagination could that be right. It took me a long time to put my finger on it, at least to my own satisfaction. And after seeing that they were the opposite of what they were supposed to be, I got extremely angry at them. I don't want to see them get away with anything. I want to see them in the penitentiary. They belong in there because they've committed so many crimes against the human rights of the people. They belong in the penitentiary!

When you focus on the adult penitentiaries, you're looking at the end of the line, trying to see where a process begins. But if you really want to understand and see what's behind the prison system, you have to look at Juvenile Hall. You have to go down to Juvenile Hall. That's where I started my career, at about the age of twelve, for some charge. I don't know what it was— vandalism. I think I ripped off a bicycle, maybe two or three bicycles. Maybe I had a bicycle business, I don't remember. But it related to bicycles. They took me to Juvenile Hall, and it took me about six months to get out again. While I was there I met a lot of people. I met a lot of *real, nice, groovy* cats who were very active, very healthy people, who had stolen bicycles and things like that. Then I moved up the ladder from Juvenile Hall to Whittier Reform School for youngsters. I graduated from there with honors and went to another one a little higher, Preston School of Industries. I graduated from that one and they jumped me up to the big leagues, to the adult penitentiary system.

I noticed that every time I went back to jail, the same guys who were in Juvenile Hall with me were also there again. They arrived there soon after I got there, or a little bit before I left. They always seemed to make the scene. In the California prison system, they carry you from Juvenile Hall to the old folks' colony, down in San Luis Obispo, and wait for you to die. Then they bury you there, if you don't have anyone outside to claim your body, and most people down there don't. I noticed these waves, these generations. I had a chance to watch other generations that came behind me, and I talked with them. I'd ask them if they'd been in jail before. You will find graduating classes moving up from Juvenile Hall, all the way up. It occurred to me that this was a social failure, one that cannot be justified by any stretch of the imagination. Not by any stretch of the imagination can the children in the Juvenile Halls be condemned, because they're innocent, and they're processed by an environment that they have no control over.

If you look at the adult prisons, you can't make head or tail out of them. By the time these men get there, they're in for murder, rape, robbery and all the high crimes. But when you look into their pasts, you find Juvenile Hall. You have to ask yourself, why is there not in this country a program for young people that will interest them? That will actively involve them and will process them to be healthy individuals leading healthy lives. Until someone answers that question for me, the only attitude I can have towards the prison system, including Juvenile Hall, is tear those walls down and let those people out of there. That's the only question. How do we tear those walls down and let those people *out* of there?

People look at the point in the Black Panther Party program that calls for freedom for all black men and women held in federal, state, county and municipal jails. They find it hard to accept that particular point. They can relate to running the police out of the community, but they say, "Those people in those prisons committed crimes. They're convicted of crimes. How can you even talk about bringing them out? If you did get them out, would you, in the black community, take them and put them on trial and send them back again?" I don't know how to deal with that. It's just no. NO! Let them out and leave them alone! Let them out because they're hip to all of us out here now. Turn them over to the Black Panther Party. Give them to us. We will redeem them from the promises of the Statue of Liberty that were never fulfilled. We have a program for them that will keep them active—twenty-four hours a day. And I don't mean eight big strong men in a big conspicuous truck robbing a jive gas station for $75.*

* Two days before this speech, eight Panthers had been arrested following a gas station robbery in San Francisco. Charges against five of them have since been dropped.

When I sit down to conspire to commit a robbery, it's going to be the Bank of America, or Chase Manhattan Bank, or Brinks.

I've been working with Bobby Seale on the biography of Huey P. Newton. Bob Scheer and I took Bobby Seale down to Carmel-by-the-Sea. But we went away from the sea. We went into a little cabin, and we got a fifth of Scotch, a couple of chasers, a tape recorder and a large stack of blank tapes. We said, "Bobby, take the fifth, and talk about brother Huey P. Newton." And Bobby started talking about Huey. One of the things that just blew my mind was when he mentioned that prior to organizing the Black Panther Party, he and Huey had been planning a gigantic bank robbery. They put their minds to work on that because they recognized that they needed money for the Movement. So they sat down and started trying to put together a key to open the vault. But as they thought about it, they thought about the implications. Bobby tells how one day while they were discussing this, Huey jumped up and said, "Later for a bank. What we're talking about is politics. What we're talking about essentially is the liberation of our people. So later for one jive bank. Let's organize the brothers and put this together. Let's arm them for defense of the black community, and it will be like walking up to the White House and saying, "Stick 'em up, motherfucker. We want what's ours."

So there's a very interesting and a very key connection between insurrection and acts carried out by oneself, a private, personal civil war. We define a civil war as when a society splits down the middle and you have two opposing sides. Does that have to be the definition? Can 5,000 people launch a civil war? Can 4,000, 3,000, two or one? Or one-half of 1,000? Or half of that? Can one person? Can one person engage in civil war? I'm not a lawyer. I'm definitely not a judge, but I would say that one person acting alone could in fact be engaged in a civil war against an oppressive system. That's how I look upon those cats in those penitentiaries. I don't care what they're in for—robbery, burglary, rape, murder, kidnap, anything. A response to a situation. A response to an environment. Any social science book will tell you that if you subject people to an unpleasant environment, you can predict that they will rebel against it. That gives rise to a contradiction. When you have a social unit organized in such a way that people are moved to rebel against it in large numbers, how, then, do you come behind them and tell them that they owe a debt to society? I say that society owes a debt to them. And society doesn't look as though it wants to pay.

There's a young brother over at Juvenile Hall in Alameda County right now by the name of Gregory Harrison. He's about fourteen or fifteen years old and he's the leader of the Black Students Union at Oakland Tech High School. At this moment they have him over there charged with insurrection. They've charged him with insurrection because the Black Students Union on that campus wants black history added to the curriculum. They want an environment created on their campus—not one that will teach black people how to be black, but one that will remove the restraints, so that they can just be themselves, and their blackness will automatically flourish. Like you don't have to teach a rose how to turn red, or teach a tree how to grow leaves.

You just leave it alone and don't pour salt on its roots, and it will be a rose, or it will be a tree.

This piggish, criminal system. This system that is the enemy of people. This very system that we live in and function in every day. This system that we are in and under at this very moment. *Our* system! Each and every one of your systems. If you happen to be from another country, it's still your system, because the system in your country is part of this. This system is *evil*. It is criminal; it is murderous. And it is in control. It is in power. It is arrogant. It is crazy. And it looks upon the people as its property. So much so that *cops*, who are public servants, feel justified in going onto a campus, a college campus or high school campus, and spraying mace in the faces of the people. They beat people with those clubs, and even shoot people, if it takes that to enforce the will of the likes of Ronald Reagan, Jesse Unruh, or Mussolini Alioto.

Have you ever seen Alioto on television? When you see him will you swear that he doesn't frighten you, or that he doesn't look like Al Capone? Alioto reminds me of convicts that I know in Folsom Prison. And this is not a contradiction. When I speak up for convicts, I don't say that every convict is going to come out here and join the Peace and Freedom Party. I'm not saying that. Or that he would be nice to people out here. I'm not saying that. Yet I call for the freedom of even those who are so alienated from society that they hate everybody. Cats who tattoo on their chest, "Born to Hate," "Born to Lose." I know a cat who tattooed across his forehead, "Born to Kill." He needs to be released also. Because whereas Lyndon B. Johnson doesn't have any tattoos on his head, he has blood dripping from his fingers. LBJ has killed more people than any man who has ever been in any prison in the United States of America from the beginning of it to the end. He has murdered. And people like prison officials, policemen, mayors, chiefs of police—they endorse it. They even call for escalation, meaning: kill more people. I don't want it. The people who are here tonight, because I see so many faces that I recognize, I could say that I know you don't want it either. There's only one way that we're going to get rid of it. That's by standing up and drawing a firm line, a distinct and firm line, and standing on our side of the line, and defending that line by whatever means necessary, including laying down our lives. Not in sacrifice, but by taking pigs with us. Taking pigs with us.

I cannot relate to spending the next four years in the penitentiary, not with madmen with supreme power in their hands. Not with Ronald Reagan the head of the Department of Corrections, as he is the head of every other state agency. Not with Dirty Red's being the warden. If they made Dr. Shapiro [San Francisco psychiatrist and long-time supporter of the Panthers] the warden of San Quentin, I'd go right now. But while they have sadistic fiends, mean men, cruel men, in control of that apparatus, I say that my interest is elsewhere. My heart is out here with the people who are trying to improve our environment.

You're even a bigger fool than I know you are if you could go through all of these abstract and ridiculous charges, all of these overt political maneuvers, and think that I'm going to relate to that. Talk all this shit that you want to, issue all the orders that you want to issue. I'm charged with a crime in Alameda County and I'm anxious to go to trial because we can deal with it. We're going to tell the truth, and the pigs are going to have to tell lies and that's hard for them to do, especially when we have with us technicians such as the Honorable Charles R. Garry [Huey Newton's attorney]. I'm not afraid to walk in any courtroom in this land with a lawyer like Garry, because he can deal with the judge and the prosecutor. But don't you come up to me telling me that you're going to revoke my parole on a charge for which I put in nine years behind the walls, and for which I was supposed to receive my discharge next month. Don't you come up to me talking that shit because I don't want to hear it.

November 22, 1968

APPENDIX

PLAYBOY INTERVIEW

WITH NAT HENTOFF

PLAYBOY: You have written that "a new black leadership with its own distinct style and philosophy will now come into its own, to center stage. Nothing can stop this leadership from taking over, because it is based on charisma, has the allegiance and support of the black masses, is conscious of its self and its position and is prepared to shoot its way to power if the need arises." As one who is increasingly regarded as among the pivotal figures in this new black leadership, how do you distinguish the new breed from those—such as Roy Wilkins and Whitney Young—most Americans consider the established Negro spokesmen?

CLEAVER: The so-called leaders you name have been willing to work within the framework of the rules laid down by the white establishment. They have tried to bring change within the system as it now is—without violence. Although Martin Luther King was the leader-spokesman for the nonviolent theme, all the rest condemn violence, too. Furthermore, all are careful to remind everybody that they're Americans as well as "Negroes," that the prestige of this country is as important to them as it is to whites. By contrast, the new black leadership identifies first and foremost with the best interests of the masses of *black* people, and we don't care about preserving the dignity of a country that has no regard for ours. We don't give a damn about any embarrassments we may cause the United States on an international level. And remember, I said the *masses* of black people. That's why we oppose Adam Clayton Powell. He's not militant enough and he represents only the black middle class, not the masses.

PLAYBOY: So far—apart from your willingness to resort to violence in achieving that goal—you haven't proposed anything specific, or different from the aims of the traditional Negro leadership.

CLEAVER: OK, the best way to be specific is to list the ten points of the Black Panther Party. They make clear that we are not willing to accept the rules of the white establishment. One: We want freedom; we want power to determine the destiny of our black communities. Two: We want full employment for our people. Three: We want housing fit for the shelter of human beings. Four: We want all black men to be exempt from military service. Five: We want decent education for black people—education that teaches us the true nature of this decadent, racist society and that teaches young black brothers and sisters their rightful place in society; for if they don't know their place in society and the world, they can't relate to anything else. Six: We want an end to the robbery of black people in their own communities by white-racist businessmen. Seven: We want an immediate end to police brutality and murder of black people. Eight: We want all black men held in city, county, state and federal jails to be released, because they haven't had fair trials; they've been tried by all-white juries, and that's like being a Jew tried in Nazi Germany. Nine: We want black people accused of crimes to be tried by members of their peer group—a peer being one who comes from the same economic, social, religious, historical and racial community. Black people, in other words, would have to compose the jury in any trial of a black person. And ten: We want land, we want money, we want housing, we want clothing, we want education, we want justice, we want peace.

PLAYBOY: Peace? But you've written that "the genie of black revolutionary violence is here."

CLEAVER: Yes, but put that into context. I've said that war will come only if these basic demands are not met. Not just a race war, which in itself would destroy this country, but a guerrilla resistance movement that will amount to a second Civil War, with thousands of white John Browns fighting on the side of the blacks, plunging America into the depths of its most desperate nightmare on the way to realizing the American Dream.

PLAYBOY: How much time is there for these demands to be met before this takes place?

CLEAVER: What will happen—and when—will depend on the dynamics of the revolutionary struggle in the black and white communities; people are going to do what they feel they have to do as the movement takes shape and gathers strength. But how long do you expect black people, who are already fed up, to endure the continued indifference of the federal government to their needs? How long will they endure the continued escalation of police force and brutality? I can't give you an exact answer, but surely they will not wait indefinitely if their demands are not met—particularly since we think that the United States has already decided where its next campaign is going to be after the war in Vietnam is over. We think the government has already picked this new target area, and it's black America. A lot of black people are very uptight about what they see in terms of preparations for the suppression of the black liberation struggle in this country. We don't work on a timetable, but we do say that the situation is deteriorating rapidly. There have been more and more armed clashes and violent encounters with the police departments that occupy black communities. Who can tell at which point any one of the dozens of incidents that take place every day will just boil over and break out into an irrevocable war? Let me make myself clear. I don't dig violence. Guns are ugly. People are what's beautiful; and when you use a gun to kill someone, you're doing something ugly. But there are two forms of violence: violence directed at you to keep you in your place and violence to defend yourself against that suppression and to win your freedom. If our demands are not met, we will sooner or later have to make a choice between continuing to be victims or deciding to seize our freedom.

PLAYBOY: But other black militants, such as the leaders of CORE, are working now for black capitalism. They even helped draft a bill introduced in Congress last summer to set up neighborhood-controlled corporations. Federal funds would be channeled through those corporations and private firms would be given tax incentives to set up businesses in black neighborhoods— businesses that would eventually be turned over to ghetto residents through the corporations.

CLEAVER: I know. It's part of a big move across the

country to convince black people that this way, they can finally get into the economic system. But we don't feel it's going to work, because it won't go far enough and deep enough to give the masses of black people real community control of all their institutions. Remember how the War on Poverty looked on paper and how it worked out? You may recall that of all the organizations around then, it was CORE that rushed in most enthusiastically to embrace that delusion; in some cities, they formed a large part of the staff. But they didn't have the decisive control, and that's where it's at. They can call these new devices "community" corporations, but those private firms from the outside can always pull out and Congress can always cut down on the federal funds they put in, just as happened in the War on Poverty.

Fewer and fewer black people are allowing themselves now to be sucked in by all of these games. A man finally reaches a point where he sees he's been tricked over and over again, and then he moves for ultimate liberation. But for the masses to achieve that, they will have to be organized so that they can make their collective weight felt, so that they themselves make the final decisions in their communities—from control of the police department to command over all social and economic programs that have to do with them. The struggle we're in now, is on two levels—getting people together locally to implement our demands and organizing black people nationally into a unified body. We want black people to be represented by leaders of their choice who, with the power of the masses behind them, will be able to go into the political arena, set forth the desires and needs of black people and have those desires and needs acted upon.

PLAYBOY: But we repeat—isn't this already happening—at least on a small scale? There's a black mayor of Cleveland, Carl Stokes, and a black mayor of Gary, Richard Hatcher.

CLEAVER: You're talking about black personalities, not about basic changes in the system. There is a large and deepening layer of black people in this country who cannot be tricked anymore by having a few black faces put up front. Let me make this very clear. We are demanding structural changes in society, and that means a real redistribution of power, so that we have control over our own lives. Having a black mayor in the present situation doesn't begin to accomplish that. And this is a question of more than breaking out of poverty. I know there are a lot of people in this country, particularly in urban ghettos, who are going hungry, who are deprived on all levels; but, obviously, it's not a matter of rampant famine. The people we deal with in the Black Panther Party are not literally dying of hunger; they're not going around in rags. But they are people who are tired of having their lives controlled and manipulated by outsiders and by people hostile to them. They're moving into a psychological and spiritual awareness of oppression, and they won't sit still for any more of it. Where we are now is in the final stages of a process with all our cards on the table. We've learned how to play cards; we know the game and we're just not going to be tricked any more. That's what seems so difficult to get across to people.

PLAYBOY: Is it a trick, however, when Senator Eugene McCarthy, among others, says that since more and more industry and, therefore, jobs, are moving out to the suburbs, more blacks will have to move there, too, with accompanying desegregation of housing in the suburbs and massive funds for improved transportation facilities? Isn't that a sincere analysis of a current trend?

CLEAVER: We feel that a lot of these attempts to relocate black people are essentially hostile moves to break up the concentration of blacks, because in that concentration of numbers, we have potential political power. We didn't choose to be packed into ghettos, but since that's where we are, we're not going to get any real power over our lives unless we use what we have—our strength as a bloc. A lot of people in the Republican and Democratic Parties are worried about all this potential black voting power in the cities; that's why, under the guise of bettering the conditions of black people, they're trying to break us up.

PLAYBOY: But wouldn't many blacks have higher incomes and live better if they could be integrated into the suburbs?

CLEAVER: I emphasize again that until black people as a whole gain power, it's not a question of where you are geographically if you're black; it's a question of where you are psychologically. No matter where you place black people under present conditions, they'll still be powerless, still subject to the whims and decisions of the white political and economic apparatus. That's why we've got to get together and stay together —especially with the country and the Congress getting more conservative politically every day, with police forces amassing more and more arms—arms on a scale to fit an army. That's why I say the situation is deteriorating rapidly—and why I'm also far from certain that the conflict between us and those who run the system can be solved short of a civil and guerrilla war.

PLAYBOY: If this civil and guerrilla war does take

place, on what do you base your assertion that there will be "thousands of white John Browns fighting on the side of the blacks"?

CLEAVER: Because we recognize that there are a lot of white people in this country who want to see virtually a new world dawn here in North America. In the Bay Area alone, there are thousands of whites who have taken fundamental stands on certain issues, particularly on our demand to free Huey Newton. A person who can relate to that, who can move himself to understand the issues involved, is a person who has begun on a path of essential commitment. Many of these people have broken with the establishment by confronting the establishment. As a situation develops in which hostilities may increase to the point of war, they will have to make a decision on which way they want to move. A certain number of them can be expected to draw back and throw their hand in; but we think there is a hard core of whites, particularly young whites, who are very alarmed at the course this country is taking. They recognize that more than freedom for blacks is at issue; their *own* freedom is at stake. They've learned this at the hands of brutal police in many, many demonstrations, including what happened at the Democratic Convention in Chicago. They've been beaten, maced, teargassed. They themselves have now experienced what's been happening to black people for so long, and they are prepared to draw the line. Previously, they recognized abstractly that this kind of suppression takes place in black communities, but they never thought it could be done to them. They are turning into a revolutionary force, and that's why we believe the Black Panthers can enter into coalitions with them as equal partners.

PLAYBOY: When and if it comes to the possibility of large-scale violence, won't most of these essentially middle-class whites—even those you call the hard core—retreat?

CLEAVER: You have to realize how deep the radicalization of young whites can become as the agents of repression against both them and us intensify their efforts. It's inevitable that the police, in order to suppress black militants, will also have to try to destroy the base of their support in the white community. When they arrest a black leader of the liberation struggle, they will also have to deal with the protests and the exposure of what they've done in certain white communities; and as they do, they will radicalize more whites. The forces of repression can no longer move just against black people. They cannot, let us say, put black people in concentration camps and simultaneously allow whites who are just as passionately involved in the liberation struggle to run around loose. There are already a lot of whites who will go to any lengths to aid their black comrades. We know this. Certainly, they must be a minority at this time; but the police, the pigs, are our best organizers for additional allies. Unwittingly, by their brutality against whites as well as blacks, they are going to keep helping us recruit more white allies who will not retreat; and that's why I don't have any doubts that we'll have thousands of new white John Browns in the future, if it comes to the point of mass revolt.

You see, whites in America really love this country. Especially young white idealists. They've always been taught that they're living in the freest country in the world, the fairest country in the world, a country that will always move to support the underdog. So when they see their government murdering people in Vietnam, the outrage flowing from that realization is immeasurable. They don't storm the Pentagon immediately; but at a distance, they begin to focus on what's really going on. People go through various stages of shock after a first awareness; they get angry, then they get uptight and finally they want to do something to change what's going on. A lot of whites have already made a correct analysis of the situation: They're aware that the government of their country has been usurped and is in the hands of a clique, what Eisenhower called the military-industrial complex, which manages the political system for the protection of the large corporations. Having made that analysis, there are enough people right now, I believe, who are so outraged at the way things are going that they would move against this usurpation if they knew how.

PLAYBOY: And how is that?

CLEAVER: That's the issue and the dilemma—how to find a revolutionary mode of moving in this most complicated of all situations. The people who supported McCarthy found out *that* wasn't the way. I'm not saying we, the Black Panthers, have the answer, either, but we're trying to find the way. One thing we do know is that we have to bring a lot of these loosely connected elements of opposition into an organizational framework. You can't have an amorphous thing pulling in all directions and realistically call it a "revolutionary movement." That's why we're organizing among blacks and intend the Panthers to be *the* black-national movement. At the same time, it makes no sense to holler for freedom for the black community and have no interconnection with white groups who also recognize the need for fundamental change. It's by coalition that we intend to bring together all the elements for liberation—by force, if all the alternatives are exhausted.

PLAYBOY: Are they exhausted, in your opinion?

CLEAVER: Not yet, but time is running out. It may still be possible, barely possible, to revolutionize this society—to get fundamental structural changes—without resorting to civil war, but only if we get enough power before it's too late.

PLAYBOY: If you fail in this last effort to effect wholesale social reform without violence, what makes you think you'll have any more success in an armed insurrection? Considering the enormously superior force and firepower of police and troops—and their apparent massive support among whites—is it realistic to believe that you can sustain a guerrilla war?

CLEAVER: Guerrilla warfare has traditionally been conceived and developed to deal with exactly this kind of situation—the presence of massive occupying forces on the one hand and the existence, on the other hand, of sizable numbers of people who are not going to confront those forces full-face but who will strike swiftly at times and places of their own choosing. Works on guerrilla warfare have been widely circulated, and a lot of people understand that it doesn't take millions of people to undermine the stability of the American economic system in that way. That's what's at stake— the stability of the system. Of course, there will be tragedies, if it comes to guerrilla warfare. On the in- dividual level, people will suffer, people will be killed. But on the mass level, more and more will be educated. It is the government itself that will become the chief agent of this kind of education, for the thrust now is unmistakably toward increasing repression. That creates an endless chain of suspicion; everyone in dissent, black or white, becomes suspect. And if the government intensifies the suppression of dissent, it cannot help but eventually become totalitarian. It creates and implements its own domino theory to the point where there won't even be lip service paid any more to individual civil liberties for black *or* white.

PLAYBOY: Police and federal agencies have shown great skill in infiltrating radical movements—including the Panthers. If conditions became such that you decided guerrilla warfare was the only alternative, isn't it likely that your group and all its potential allies— with or without the help of black veterans—would be instantly neutralized from within, because the government would know every move you planned?

CLEAVER: As for the Panthers, we have always worked on the assumption that we're under constant surveillance and have long been infiltrated. But we figure this is something you just have to live with. In any case, the destruction of a particular organization will not destroy the will to freedom among any oppressed people. Nor will it destroy the certainty that they'll act to win it. Sure, we try to take precautions to make sure we're not including hostile elements in our organization, but we don't spend all our time worrying about it. If we go under—and that could easily be done with police frame-ups right now—there'll be others to take our place.

PLAYBOY: Have you considered the possibility that you could be wrong about the chances of waging a successful guerrilla war? Don't you run the risk that all your efforts toward that end—even if they don't escalate beyond rhetoric—could invite a massive wave of repression that would result in a black blood-bath and turn the country's ghettos into concentration camps?

CLEAVER: It seems to me a strange assumption that black people could just be killed or cooped up into concentration camps and that would be the end of it. This isn't the 1930's. We're not going to play Jews. The whole world is different now from what it was then. Not only would black people resist, with the help of white people, but we would also have the help of those around the world who are just waiting for some kind of extreme crisis within this country so that they can move for their own liberation from American repression abroad. This government does not have unlimited forces of repression; it can't hold the whole world down—not at home *and* abroad. Eventually, it will be able to control the racial situation here only by ignoring its military "commitments" overseas. That might stop *our* movement for a while, but think what would be happening in Latin America, Asia and Africa. In that event, there would be a net gain for freedom in the world. We see our struggle as inextricably bound up with the struggle of all oppressed peoples, and there is no telling what sacrifices we in this country may have to make before that struggle is won.

PLAYBOY: Do you think you have any real chance of winning that struggle—even without government repression—as long as the majority of white Americans, who outnumber blacks ten to one, remain hostile or indifferent to black aspirations? According to the indications of recent public-opinion surveys, they deplore even *nonviolent* demonstrations on behalf of civil rights.

CLEAVER: At the present stage, the majority of

white people are indifferent and complacent simply because their own lives have remained more or less intact and as remote from the lives of most blacks as the old French aristocracy was from "the great unwashed." It's disturbing to them to hear about Hough burning, Watts burning, the black community in Newark burning. But they don't really understand why it's happening, and they don't really care, as long as *their* homes and *their* places of work—or the schools to which they send their children—aren't burning, too. So for most whites, what's happened up to now has been something like a spectator sport. There may be a lot more of them than there are of us, but they're not really involved; and there are millions and millions of black people in this country who *are*—more than the census shows. Maybe 30 million, maybe more. A lot of black people never get counted in the census. It's not going to be easy to deal with that large a number, and it won't be possible to indefinitely limit the burning to black neighborhoods—even with all the tanks, tear gas, riot guns, paddy wagons and fire trucks in this country. But if it does come to massive repression of blacks, I don't think the majority of whites are going to either approve it or remain silent. If a situation breaks out in which soldiers are hunting down and killing black people obviously and openly, we don't think the majority will accept that for long. It could go on for a while, but at some point, we think large numbers of whites would become so revolted that leaders would arise in the white community and offer other solutions. So we don't accept the analysis that we're doomed because we're in a minority. We don't believe that the majority in this country would permit concentration camps and genocide.

PLAYBOY: Not even in the midst of large-scale violence in which white neighborhoods were being burned and looted, white children being endangered?

CLEAVER: Under those circumstances, it might be very possible for the power structure to capitalize sufficiently on white fear and anger to justify such atrocities even against those not involved in the violence. But there would still be elements in the white community that would resist massive and indiscriminate repression of all blacks; and once the immediate causes of fear and anger were over, I believe the majority would begin to protest and eventually move against mass imprisonment and genocide. I'm not saying most white people don't have racist attitudes. They do, because the values taught in this country inevitably result in whites' having racist attitudes. But I think a lot of whites are made racists against their essential humanity and without their conscious knowledge. And they get very uncomfortable when their actions are identified as racist even by their own Kerner Commission. They would really be put on the spot if a large-scale confrontation took place between black people as a whole and white people as a whole. In that event, a lot of white people could not endure seeing themselves as part of the totalitarian apparatus. They would make it very clear that they opposed it and they would work to stop it—not only because of their essential humanity but because it would be in their own self-interest. The United States has huge interests to safeguard around the world, and most whites would recognize how seriously those interests would be jeopardized if there was total suppression of blacks domestically. That's another reason why the fact of our numerical minority doesn't mean we're destined to lose in our struggle for freedom. It doesn't take into account the international context of the black-liberation movement here. If this country's power structure was really free to totally, brutally and openly suppress black people at home, it would have done so a long time ago. So we have more going for us than our numbers; and our numbers are getting larger.

PLAYBOY: Suppose you're right in claiming that most whites, for whatever reason, would not support massive repression of blacks in this country. These same whites, however, don't want black violence, either—but as you point out, most don't fully grasp the dimensions of the injustices against which that violence is a rebellion, nor do they understand why it continues in the wake of several milestone civil rights laws and Supreme Court decisions. The familiar question is: "What more do they want?" How would you answer it?

CLEAVER: I can only answer with what Malcolm X said. If you've had a knife in my back for four hundred years, am I supposed to thank you for pulling it out? Because that's all those laws and decisions have accomplished. The very least of your responsibility now is to compensate me, however inadequately, for centuries of degradation and disenfranchisement by granting peacefully—before I take them forcefully—the same rights and opportunities for a decent life that you've taken for granted as an American birthright. This isn't a request but a *demand,* and the ten points of that demand are set down with crystal clarity in the Black Panther Party platform.

PLAYBOY: Many would doubt that you're serious about some of them. Point four, for instance: "We want all black men to be exempt from military service."

CLEAVER: We couldn't be more serious about that point. As a colonized people, we consider it absurd to fight the wars of the mother country against other colonized peoples, as in Vietnam right now. The conviction that no black man should be forced to fight for the system that's suppressing him is growing among more and more black people, outside the Black Panther Party as well as in it. And as we can organize masses of black people behind that demand for exemption, it will have to be taken seriously.

PLAYBOY: Are you equally serious about point eight, which demands that all black prisoners held in city, county, state and federal jails be released because they haven't had fair trials; and about point nine, which demands that the black defendants be tried by all-black juries?

CLEAVER: We think the day will come when these demands, too, will receive serious attention, because they deserve it. Take point eight. All the social sciences —criminology, sociology, psychology, economics—point out that if you subject people to deprivation and inhuman living conditions, you can predict that they will rebel against those conditions. What we have in this country is a system organized against black people in such a way that many are forced to rebel and turn to forms of behavior that are called criminal in order to get the things they need to survive. Consider the basic contradiction here. You subject people to conditions that make rebellion inevitable and then you punish them for rebelling. Now, under those circumstances, does the black convict owe a debt to society or does society owe a debt to the black convict? Since the social, economic and political system is so rigged against black people, we feel the burden of the indictment should rest on the system and not on us. Therefore, black people should not be confined in jails and prisons for rebelling against that system—even though the rebellion might express itself in some unfortunate ways. And this idea can be taken further, to apply also to those white people who have been subjected to a disgusting system for so long that they resort to disgusting forms of behavior. This is part of our fundamental critique of the way this society, under its present system of organization, molds the character of its second-class citizens.

PLAYBOY: Have you considered the consequences to society of opening the prisons and setting all the inmates free? Their behavior may in one sense be society's fault, but they're still criminals.

CLEAVER: We don't feel that there's any black man or any white man in any prison in this country who could be compared in terms of criminality with Lyndon Johnson. No mass murderer in any penitentiary in America or in any other country comes anywhere close to the thousands and thousands of deaths for which Johnson is responsible.

PLAYBOY: Do you think that analogy is valid? After all, Johnson has been waging a war, however misguidedly, in the belief that his cause is just.

CLEAVER: Many murderers feel exactly the same way about *their* crimes. But let me give you another example: Compare the thieves in our prisons with the big-businessmen of this country, who are in control of a system that is depriving millions of people of a decent life. These people—the men who run the government and the corporations—are much more dangerous than the guy who walks into a store with a pistol and robs somebody of a few dollars. The men in control are robbing the entire world of billions and billions of dollars.

PLAYBOY: *All* the men in control?

CLEAVER: That's what I said: and they're not only stealing money, they're robbing people of life itself. When you talk about criminals, you have to recognize the vastly different degrees of criminality.

PLAYBOY: Surely no criminality, proved in a court of law, should go unpunished.

CLEAVER: As you know, the poor and the black in this country don't seem to make out as well as the rich and the white in our courts of "justice." I wonder why.

PLAYBOY: You still haven't answered our question about the social consequences of releasing all those now behind bars.

CLEAVER: Those who are now in prison could be put through a process of real rehabilitation before their release—not caged like animals, as they are now, thus guaranteeing that they'll be hardened criminals when they get out if they weren't when they went in. By rehabilitation I mean they would be trained for jobs that would not be an insult to their dignity, that would give them some sense of security, that would allow them to achieve some brotherly connection with their fellow man. But for this kind of rehabilitation to happen on a large scale would entail the complete reorganization of society, not to mention the prison system. It would call for the teaching of a new set of ethnics, based on the principle of cooperation, as opposed to the presently dominating principle of competition. It would require the transformation of the entire moral fabric of this country into a way of being that would make these former criminals feel more obligated to their fellow man than they do now. The way things are today, however, what reasons do these victims of society have for feeling an obligation to their fellow man? I look with respect on a guy who has walked the streets because he's been unable to find a job in a system that's rigged against him, who doesn't go around begging and instead walks into a store and says, "Stick 'em up, motherfucker!" I prefer that man to the Uncle Tom who does nothing but just shrink into himself and accept any shit that's thrown into his face.

PLAYBOY: Would you feel that way if it were *your* store that got held up?

CLEAVER: That's inconceivable; I wouldn't own a store. But for the sake of argument, let's say I did. I'd still respect the guy who came in and robbed me more than the panhandler who mooched a dime from me in the street.

PLAYBOY: But would you feel he was *justified* in robbing you because of his disadvantaged social background?

CLEAVER: Yes, I would—and this form of social rebellion is on the rise. When I went to San Quentin in 1958, black people constituted about 30 per cent of the prison population. Recently, I was back at San Quentin, and the blacks are now in the majority. There's an incredible number of black people coming in with each new load of prisoners. Moreover, I've talked to a lot of other people who've been in different prisons, and the percentage of black inmates there, too, is indisputably climbing. And within that growing number, the percentage of *young* black prisoners is increasing most of all. Youngsters from the ages of eighteen to twenty-three are clearly in the majority of the new people who come to prison. The reason is that for a lot of black people, including the young, jobs are almost nonexistent, and the feeling of rebellion is particularly powerful among the young. Take a guy who was four years old in 1954, when the Supreme Court decision on school desegregation was handed down, a decision that was supposed to herald a whole new era. Obviously, it didn't, but it did accelerate agitation and unrest. So this guy, who was four then, has had a lifetime of hearing grievances articulated very sharply but of seeing nothing changed. By the time he's eighteen or nineteen, he's very, very uptight. He's very turned off to the system and he has it in his mind that he's justified in moving against so unjust a system in any way he sees fit.

PLAYBOY: Can that be the whole explanation for the growing number of young black prisoners? Are they all in conscious rebellion against the white power structure?

CLEAVER: That's not the whole explanation, of course, but it would be a mistake to underestimate that rising mood of rebellion. Whatever their conscious motivation, though, every one of them is in prison because of the injustice of society itself. White people are able to get away with a lot of things black people can't begin to get away with; cops are much quicker to make busts in black neighborhoods. And even when they're arrested, whites are ahead because more of them can afford attorneys. A lot of black cats end up in prison solely because they didn't have someone to really present their cases in court. They're left with the public defenders, whom prison inmates quite accurately call "penitentiary deliverers." I'll tell you what usually happens. It's the common practice of the police to file ten or so charges on you, and then the public defender comes and says, "Look, we can't beat them all, so the best thing you can do is plead guilty on one count. If you do that, I can get the others dropped." So a black cat is sitting there without real legal help, without any money, and he knows that if he's convicted of all ten counts, he'll get a thousand years. He's in a stupor of confusion and winds up taking the advice of the public defender. He doesn't know the law. He doesn't know how to make legal motions. He doesn't really know what's going on in that courtroom. So he goes along, wakes up in the penitentiary, starts exchanging experiences with other guys who have been through the same mill; and if he wasn't a rebel when he went in, he'll be a revolutionary by the time he gets out.

PLAYBOY: What happens to the ordinary black inmate who has no special talent that earns him a reputation—and influential supporters—outside of prison?

CLEAVER: When I was in the guidance center at San Quentin last spring, I saw a lot of people like that—people I've known for years. Two of them had been in Los Angeles Juvenile Hall with me the first time I was ever arrested—some eighteen years ago. Since then, they had done some time and been paroled, and here they were back in San Quentin on bullshit charges of parole violation. That's a device used all the time to keep sending people back to prison. These guys had done nothing more than have personality clashes with their parole officers, who were empowered to send them back up on their own arbitrary decision. This would never have happened if these guys had had any decent legal help. But neither had anybody outside but their mothers and fathers. And they were just two among hundreds of kids in that guidance center who'd been sent back on parole violations, for no better reason. They hadn't committed felonies; they hadn't done anything that would get the average white man hauled into court. The only conclusion one can draw is that the parole system is a procedure devised primarily for the purpose of running people in and out of jail—most of them black—in order to create and maintain a lot of jobs for the white prison system. In California, which I know best—and I'm sure it's the same in other states—there are thousands and thousands of people who draw their living directly or indirectly from the prison system: all the clerks, all the guards, all the bailiffs, all the people who sell goods to the prisons. They regard the inmates as a sort of product from which they all draw their livelihood, and the part of the crop they keep exploiting most are the black inmates.

PLAYBOY: And one of the ways you propose to solve this problem is by demanding not only that all black people in prisons be released but that all future trials of blacks be judged by all-black juries. Wouldn't the selection of a jury on the basis of color—whatever the motivation—be at variance with the U.S. Constitution?

CLEAVER: The Constitution says very little explicitly; it has to be interpreted. Given the racism in this country and the inability of white people to understand what's going on with black people, the only truly just way for a black man to be tried by his peers is for him to have a jury of people who have been victims of the same socioeconomic and political situations *he* has experienced.

PLAYBOY: By the same process of reasoning, wouldn't it follow that a member of the Ku Klux Klan accused of murdering a civil rights worker should be

tried only by an all-white jury of Southern segregation-
ists because only they would have backgrounds similar
enough to understand his motivations?

CLEAVER: That's pretty much the way it happens,
as a matter of fact. But I don't think the majority of
whites will be content for too long with that kind of
Ku Klux Klan subversion of justice. My primary concern, in any case, is justice for black people *by* black
people; if we can achieve that, then we might be ready
to talk about whether blacks and whites could get together in accomplishing real justice across the board.
But in our *present* society, the only way the Constitution can mean anything to blacks in terms of justice is
for black people to be tried by their black peers.

PLAYBOY: You seem to alternate between advocating
revolutionary violence and allowing for the possibility
of social reform without violence. Which is it going to
be?

CLEAVER: What happens, as I've said, will depend on
the continuing dynamics of the situation. What we're
doing now is telling the government that if it does not
do its duty, then we will see to it ourselves that justice is
done. Again, I can't tell you when we may have to start
defending ourselves by violence from continued violence
against us. That will depend on what is done against us
and on whether real change can be accomplished nonviolently within the system. We'd much rather do it that
way, because we don't feel it would be a healthy situation to have even black revolutionaries going around
distributing justice. I'd much prefer a society in which
we wouldn't have to use—or even carry—guns, but that
means the pigs would have to be disarmed, too. In the
meantime, as long as this remains an unjust and unsafe

society for black people, we're faced with a situation in which our survival is at stake. We will do whatever we must to protect our lives and to redeem the lives of our people—without too much concern for the niceties of a system that is rigged against us.

PLAYBOY: Some black militants say there is an alternative to revolution or capitulation: the formation of a separate black nation within the United States. At a meeting in Detroit last March, a group of black nationalists proposed the creation of a state called New Africa, encompassing all the territory now occupied by Alabama, Georgia, Louisiana, Mississippi and South Carolina. Do you think that's a viable plan?

CLEAVER: I don't have any sympathy with that approach, but the Black Panthers feel that it's a proposal black people should be polled on. There have been too many people and too many organizations in the past who claimed to speak for the ultimate destiny of black people. Some call for a new state; some have insisted that black people should go back to Africa. We Black Panthers, on the other hand, don't feel we should speak for all black people. We say that black people deserve an opportunity to record their own national will.

PLAYBOY: Few, if any, colonized peoples have the support of a contingent of the colonizing power; yet the Black Panthers have formed a working coalition with the Peace and Freedom Party in California—a group that is predominantly white. Isn't there an ideological inconsistency in such a coalition—despite what you've said about the good will and dedication of many sympathetic young whites—at a time when other militant black organizations, such as SNCC, pointedly reject all white allies as agents of the white power structure?

CLEAVER: There is no inconsistency if you don't confuse coalitions with mergers. We believe black people should be in full control of their organizations; the Black Panthers have always been. You may remember that Stokely Carmichael, when he came out for an all-black SNCC, also said that the role of whites was to go into their own communities and organize, so that there could be a basis for eventual coalitions. We've now reached a point where many white people have, in fact, organized in their own communities; therefore, we see no reason to maintain an alienated posture and to refuse to work with such groups.

PLAYBOY: One of the passages in *Soul on Ice* had particular impact on many young white people who felt they had been drummed out of "the movement." You wrote: "There is in America today a generation of white youth that is truly worthy of a black man's respect, and this is a rare event in the foul annals of American history." Having since worked in collaboration with the Peace and Freedom Party, do you still think as highly of the new generation of white youth?

CLEAVER: I'm even more convinced it's true than when I wrote those lines. We work with these young people all the time, and we've had nothing but encouraging experiences with them. These young white people aren't hung up battling to maintain the status quo like some of the older people who think they'll become extinct if the system changes. They're adventurous: they're willing to experiment with new forms; they're willing to confront life. And I don't mean only those on college campuses. A lot who aren't in college share with their college counterparts an ability to welcome and work for change.

PLAYBOY: Do you agree with those who feel that

this generation of youth is going to "sell out" to the status quo as it moves into middle age?

CLEAVER: I expect all of us will become somewhat less resilient as we get into our forties and fifties—if we live that long—and I'm sure that those who come after us will look back on us as being conservative. Even us Panthers. But I don't think this generation will become as rigid as the ones before; and, for that matter, I don't write off all older people right now. There are a lot of older whites and blacks who keep working for change. So there are people over thirty I trust. *I'm* over thirty, and I trust *me*.

PLAYBOY: You speak of trust, and yet there are many young whites—despite what you've said—who wonder if black people are really willing to trust them and to work with them on a basis of mutual respect. Bobby Seale, a Black Panther leader, for instance, told an audience of young whites in New York last spring: "We hate you white people! And the next time one of you paddies comes up here and accuses me of hating you because of the color of your skin, I will kick you in your ass. We started *out* hating you because of the color of your skin. . . . In school, when a little white liberal walked by, I used to come up with my knife and say, 'Give me your lunch money or I'll cut your guts out.' And he'd give me his lunch money. Pretty soon, I'd say, 'Tomorrow you bring me two dollars.' And the next day he'd bring me two dollars. Because that two dollars was mine. Mine because of four hundred years of racism and oppression. When I take two dollars from you, pig, don't you say nothing." What kind of white person, unless he's a masochist, could form a coalition with black people on this basis?

CLEAVER: I heard about that speech. There's been

a lot of reaction to it, and it's unfortunate. As I understand it, Bobby had been preceded on that program by LeRoi Jones and a lot of that kind of thing, and maybe Bobby was turned on by all that. I don't know. But I do know Bobby; and if that quote is correct, it does not represent how he really feels—not deep inside. You have to remember that Bobby Seale, with Huey Newton, laid the foundation for the Black Panthers; and it was because of their attitudes that the party has been able to steer clear of getting involved in any of these dead-end racist positions. If you go around and talk to the white people in the Bay Area who have worked with Bobby, you'll find that they know the real Bobby Seale and are not disturbed by what he might have said on one particular occasion. It's even fair to say that a lot of them love Bobby. When that particular speech was made, I was in jail; but I've talked with Bobby about it since, and I don't condemn him for it.

PLAYBOY: As you know, however, there are many who do and who believe he really meant what he said that night. In reaction to his and Jones' remarks, one young white radical wrote in *Rat Subterranean News*, the underground New York biweekly: "You are denying my humanity and my individuality. Though I am in deepest empathy with you and with all blacks—all people—in their struggle to be free, you are in danger of becoming my enemy. I must revolt against your racism, your scorn of everything white, just as I revolt against the racism of white America. I will not let you put me in a bag. Your enemies and my enemies are the same people, the same institutions. . . . I feel no special loyalty to White, but only Self. I feel no love for the leaders or institutions or culture of this country, but only for individual people, in an ever-growing number, with whom I share love and trust. I deny my whiteness; I affirm my humanity. You are urging your black brothers to see me only as White, in just the same way as we have been raised to see you only as Negro. . . . I don't feel white enough or guilty enough to die joyfully by a bullet from a black man's gun, crying 'Absolved at last!' And I know that soon *you,* by denying me my me-ness, will become for me just as much an oppressor, just as much an enemy, as the white culture we are both fighting. . . . To remain free, and to transform society, I have to maintain my hard-won differentiation from the mass of white people, and I won't let even a black person, no matter how hard-bent he be on black liberation, squeeze me back into honkiedom. If I have to shoot a black racist one of these days, well, baby, that's part of the struggle." This rejection of racism has been echoed by many young whites. What's your reaction to it?

CLEAVER: I think it's a commendable statement. But there are many whites who do deny the humanity of black people, and I think LeRoi and Bobby were talking about them. If you're white and you don't fall into that bag, though, there is no reason why you should accept that analysis as applying to you. You have to judge people by what they do. Those white people who are still functioning as part of the juggernaut of oppression are, indeed, guilty. But those who place themselves outside the system of oppression, those who struggle against that system, ought not to consider that judgment applied against them. I think when a person has reached the kind of awareness expressed by this cat, he is totally justified in rebelling against the honkie tag. But he ought not to expect some kind of instant recognition

by black people that he's "different." You cannot expect
black people to make immediate distinctions while
blacks themselves are still involved in the total fabric of
oppression. Those whites who have freed themselves of
the system know who they are; by what they do, *we* will
get to know who they are.

PLAYBOY: Specifically, what can they do, what must
they do, to earn your respect and trust?

CLEAVER: There are a whole lot of things they can
do. They can organize white people so that together we
can go into the halls of government, demand our rights
—and get them. They can organize politically and get
rid of all the clods and racists in the legislatures around
the country. They can help keep the police from rioting.
They can help make public servants recognize that they
are public servants, that the public—black and white—
pays their salaries and that they don't own the people
and must be responsive to them. What can whites do?
Just be Americans, as the rhetoric claims Americans are
supposed to be. Just stand up for liberty everywhere.
Stand up for justice everywhere—especially right here
in their own country. Stand up for the underdog; that's
supposed to be the American way. Make this *really* the
home of the free. But that will never happen unless they
help us conduct a thorough housecleaning of the political and economic arenas. Now is the time for whites
to help us get the machinery together, to organize themselves and then form coalitions with black groups and
Mexican and Puerto Rican groups that also want to
bring about social change—and then act to do just that.

PLAYBOY: What about whites—undoubtedly a much
larger number—who are just not revolutionaries but
still want to work for positive change?

CLEAVER: That's simple, too. Find out which white organizations are for real and join them. Many whites can help educate other whites about the true nature of the system. And they can help black people—in the courts, in the social clubs, in the Congress, in the city councils, in the board rooms—win their demands for justice. The number-one problem right now, as we see it, is that of repression by the police. Whites should become aware of what the police are doing and why the Black Panther Party, to name only one group, has got so hung-up over this crucial question. It's not just police brutality and crimes; it's police intimidation of black communities. When we started, it became very clear to us that the reason black people don't come out to meetings, don't join organizations working for real change, is that they're afraid of various forms of retaliation from the police. They're afraid of being identified as members of a militant organization. So we recognized that the first thing we had to do was to expose and deal with the Gestapo power of the police. Once we've done that, we can move to mobilize people who will then be free to come out and start discussing and articulating their grievances, as well as proposing various changes and solutions. We are doing that in the Bay Area and in other areas where the Black Panther Party is now active. But there are many places where the police continue to intimidate, and it would be a great help for white people to start their own local organizations or to form local chapters of the Peace and Freedom Party. They could then focus community attention on what the police actually do—as opposed to what the police and the city administrations *claim* they do—and work with black people who are trying to break free.

That kind of organized activity is really the only hope for this country.

PLAYBOY: If whites were to do this, wouldn't they have a lot to lose, even if they themselves don't become the victims of police repression? Radicals keep telling them that if they're really going to join in the struggle, they can't go on living as they do now; that they can't expect to continue enjoying the material comforts of a system they intend to confront; that anyone who "breaks free" is going to have to change his entire style of life. Do you agree?

CLEAVER: Well, they're certainly going to have to give up those privileges that are based on the oppression and exploitation of other people. Most whites today are in the position of being the recipients of stolen property. This country was *built,* in large part, on the sweat of slaves. The standard of living most white people enjoy today is a direct result of the historical exploitation of blacks, and of the Third World, by the imperialist nations, of which America is now the leader. But thanks to technological advances, even if that exploitation were stopped and there were just distribution of wealth abroad and at home, whites wouldn't really have to suffer materially. If the money now used for bombs and airplanes were redirected to build more houses and better schools—as even the white man's Kerner Commission recommended—I can't see how white people would have to make any sacrifices at all. And think of how much more wholesome—and peaceful—a social environment there'd be for everybody. It seems to me the only whites who would be losing anything are those irretrievably committed, emotionally or economically, to the continued subordination of nonwhites. But those whites who are not wedded to exploitation and oppression can only benefit if basic change comes.

PLAYBOY: There are whites who would say that black people have not indicated that they have the determination, the discipline or even the good will to work toward such a goal. As you know, many privately feel that black people, with some exceptions, are lazy, irresponsible, destructive rather than constructive, unable to hold onto jobs, etc., etc. How do you think this problem of noncomprehension and lingering prejudice can be overcome?

CLEAVER: Well, insofar as any of these stereotypes seem to have some basis in fact, they're the result of *strategic* forms of behavior by black people. Think about that. I don't see any reason, for instance, why black people should have been knocking themselves out on the plantations. Under slavery, the black man who could find ways to get out of work was really a very wise man. It's no different under the present system of exploitation, a system rigged against black people straight across the board. Why should any black man strive to excel, to better himself, when the system is set up to keep him "in his place"? I think anyone who can beat that system and draw a living from it with the least expenditure of energy is doing the best thing he can do for himself. It's stupid to be a dedicated, hardworking and loyal victim. But if black people were in a situation where their labor had meaning and dignity, where they were really building good lives for themselves and their children, then all this strategic behavior would cease to be functional.

PLAYBOY: That answer might help convince some

potential white allies of the viability of a black-white coalition for change. But how do you reconcile such expressions of hope with a statement you wrote for *Ramparts* shortly after the murder of Martin Luther King? "There is a holocaust coming . . . the war has begun. The violent phase of the black liberation struggle is here, and it will spread. From that shot, from that blood, America will be painted red. Dead bodies will litter the streets and the scenes will be reminiscent of the disgusting, terrifying, nightmarish news reports coming out of Algeria during the height of the general violence right before the final breakdown of the French colonial regime." If you really believe that, what's the point of talking about black-white coalitions?

CLEAVER: Let me emphasize again that I try to be realistic. I keep working for change, in the hope that violence will not be necessary; but I cannot pretend, in the face of the currently deteriorating situation, that a holocaust is not very possible, even likely. Perhaps if enough people recognize how possible it is, they'll work all the harder for the basic changes that can prevent it. Obviously, there have already been dead bodies on the streets since the murder of King; and at some point, there can occur an eruption that will escalate beyond control. But let me also make clear that I do not justify shooting the wrong people. If the holocaust comes, the bodies on the streets would be those of the oppressors: those who control the corporations that profiteer off the poor, that oil the war machine, that traffic with racist nations like South Africa; those who use the economic and military power of the U.S. to exploit and exterminate the disenfranchised in this country and around the world; and, above all, those politicians who use their public trust to kill social reform and perpetuate in-justice. The rest are just part of the machinery. They're not making decisions. They're not manipulating the masses. They're being manipulated themselves by the criminals who run the country.

PLAYBOY: And these "criminals" are to be killed if there's a violent revolution?

CLEAVER: It seems to be a hallmark of any revolutionary war that the worst culprits are stood up against the wall and executed. There are a lot of people in the category of active oppressor for whom I think execution would be a mild punishment. However, given an ideal situation, it might be possible to incarcerate these people, re-educate them and then allow them back into society, if they're not actually guilty of willful murder. But in the heat of a violent day-to-day struggle, one might not have time to be so fastidious with these people; in that event, anything that's done to them would be all right with me.

PLAYBOY: In everything you say, there are the intertwining themes of vengeance and forgiveness, of violent revolution and nonviolent social reform; and that leads to a good deal of confusion among many whites as to what the Black Panthers are really for. On the one hand, you write of the coming holocaust and of bodies littering the streets. And yet the day before you wrote that article, you were at a junior high school in Oakland, where the black kids had decided to burn down the school in anger at the murder of Dr. King, and you talked them out of it. Similarly, you and other Panthers speak of a black revolutionary generation that has the courage to kill; yet when a group of seventh and eighth graders at another Oakland school tried to emulate what they thought the Panthers stood for by turning into a gang and beating up other kids, several Panther leaders went to the school at the invitation of the principal and told the kids they were in the wrong bag. The Panthers' advice was for black youngsters to study hard, so that they could be in a better position to help their brothers. They also told them not to hate whites but to learn to work with them. Which is the *real* Black Panther philosophy?

CLEAVER: There is no contradiction between what we say and what we do. We are for responsible action. That's why we don't advocate people going around inventing hostilities and burning down schools and thereby depriving youngsters of a place to learn. What we do advocate is that hostilities in the black community be focused on specific targets. The police are a specific target. As I said before, we are engaged in organizing black communities so that they will have the power to stop the police from wanton harassment and killing of black people. And that also means self-defense, if necessary. Beyond that, it means getting enough power so that we can have autonomous black departments of safety in black communities. We have the courage—and the good sense—to defend ourselves, but we are not about to engage in the kind of random violence that will give the pigs an opportunity to destroy us. We are revolutionary, but that means we're disciplined, that we're working out programs, that we intend to create a radical political machinery in coalition with whites that will uproot this decadent society, transform its politics and economics and build a structure fit to exist on a civilized planet inhabited by *humanized* beings.

PLAYBOY: You say the police are a prime target for

Panther hostility. Is this, perhaps, because the reverse is also true? Police departments in all the cities in which the Panthers have organized claim that your group is a public menace—engaged in beatings, shakedowns, thefts, shootings, fire bombings and other criminal activities.

CLEAVER: Who are the criminals? I know about these rumors of what Panthers are supposed to be doing, but that's all they are—false reports spread by racist cops. They'd like the public to forget that it was Black Panthers in Brooklyn who were attacked by off-duty *police* outside a courtroom last September. Who were the criminals there? And who shot up the Black Panther office in Oakland in a drunken orgy, riddling pictures of Huey Newton and me—and a picture of Bobby Hutton, whom they had already killed? Two pigs from the Oakland Police Department. Of course, they're going to spread these false rumors about us; it's one of the ways they're trying to destroy us before we destroy them with the truth about their own lawlessness.

PLAYBOY: Granted there have been conflicts between the Panthers and the police; but aren't you exaggerating their intent when you claim, as you did recently, that they're out to "systematically eliminate our leadership"?

CLEAVER: Not in the least. We are a great threat to the police and to the whole white power structure in Alameda County and in Oakland, where the Panthers were born. The police are the agents of the power structure, in trying to destroy us. Let me give you the background. When Bobby Seale and Huey Newton organized the Black Panther Party in October 1966, they initiated armed black patrols. Each car, which had four men, would follow the police around, observing them. When police accosted a citizen on the street and started doing something wrong to him, the patrol would be there as witnesses and to tell the person being mistreated what his rights were. In this way, the Panthers focused community attention on the police and the people learned they didn't have to submit to the kind of oppressive, arbitrary brutality that had been directed against the black people in Oakland for a long time.

When the Panthers started to educate the community, those in power were afraid that blacks would go on to organize and exercise real political power. And the police were told to prevent this. They tried to do this first by multiple arrests. Anyone known to be a Panther would be rousted on ridiculous charges that couldn't stand up in court but that led to our having to spend a lot of money on bail and legal fees. That didn't work. They couldn't intimidate us. Then in October 1967, they finally got Huey Newton into a position where a shoot-out occurred. Huey was wounded, a cop was killed and another was wounded. Murder charges were filed against Huey; he was eventually convicted and sentenced to two to fifteen years, and that case is now on appeal. After the shoot-out and the arrest of Huey, the whole Black Panther Party became involved in mobilizing community awareness of the political aspects of that case.

We had such great effect in that effort that the police tried even harder to stifle us. They moved against just about everyone who had taken an active part in speaking and mobilizing for Huey. To give you some examples, on January 15 of this year, our national captain, David Hilliard, was arrested while passing out leaflets at Oakland Tech. The next day, police broke down the door of my apartment and searched it without a warrant. On February 5, a Panther and his girlfriend were arrested for "disturbing the peace" after a rally at which Dr. Spock had spoken. They were beaten in jail. On February 24, Panther Jimmy Charley approached a policeman who was assaulting a black person. He questioned the officer and was immediately arrested and charged with "resisting arrest." On February 25, at 3:30 in the morning, police broke down the door of Bobby Seale's home. Again, there was no warrant. During the third and fourth weeks of February, there was a rash of arrests of black men either in the Panthers or identified with them. And on and on.

PLAYBOY: You've also been a spokesman for the Peace and Freedom Party, of which you were this year's Presidential nominee. How significant do you consider that kind of political activity, in terms of your plans for the growth of the Black Panthers?

CLEAVER: Well, I never exactly dreamed of waking up in the White House after the November election, but I took part in that campaign because I think it's necessary to pull a lot of people together, black and white. Certainly, we're concerned with building the Black Panther Party, but we also have to build a national coalition between white activists and black activists. We have to build some machinery so that they can work on a coordinated basis. Right now, you have thousands and thousands of young activists, black and white, who are working at cross purposes, who don't communicate with one another, who are isolated and alienated from one another. But they could be a source of mutual strength and support. I believe that if we can simultaneously move forward the liberation struggle that's going on in the black colonies of this country and the revolutionary struggle that's going on in the mother country, we can amass the strength and numbers needed to change the course of American history.

PLAYBOY: There are those who believe that this vision of yours is just another of those fugitive illusions that appear from time to time among radicals, black and white. Michael Harris, a reporter for the *San Francisco Chronicle,* wrote in *The Nation* last July, quoting a law-enforcement agent who had infiltrated the Panthers: "If the federal government makes a serious effort to pump lots of money into the ghetto, you can likely kiss the Panthers goodbye. You simply can't agitate happy people." Do you think that's likely to happen?

CLEAVER: If the federal government moved to honor all the grievances of black people, not merely to alleviate but eliminate oppression, we'd be delighted to fold the whole thing up and call it a day. There are many other—and certainly safer—things we'd prefer to be doing with our lives. But until the government moves to undo all the injustices—every one of them, every last shadow of colonialism—no amount of bribes, brutality, threats or promises is going to deter us from our cause. There will be no compromise, no surrender and no sell-out; we will accept nothing less than total victory. That's why more and more black people have faith in us—because we offer a totally inflexible program in terms of our demands for black people, yet we have steered clear of doing this in a racist manner, as the Muslims have done. People are turning not to Muslims, not to the NAACP, not to CORE or SNCC but to the Black Panther Party.

PLAYBOY: Is this happening more among older people or among the young?

CLEAVER: We're getting older people, but we're acquiring particular strength in colleges, high schools, junior high schools, even grammar schools. We count very heavily on the young, in terms of the future. The Black Panther Party is a natural organization for them to join. It was organized by their peers; it understands the world the way they understand it. And for the young black male, the Black Panther Party supplies very badly needed standards of masculinity. The result is that all the young chicks in the black community nowadays relate to young men who are Black Panthers.

PLAYBOY: You seem to have undergone quite a change in attitude since you were their age, when you related not to black girls but to white women, and in a decidedly unhealthy way. In *Soul on Ice,* you wrote: "Somehow I arrived at the conclusion that, as a matter of principle, it was of paramount importance for me to have an antagonistic, ruthless attitude toward white women. . . . I had stepped outside of the white man's law, which I repudiated with scorn and self-satisfaction. I became a law unto myself—my own legislature, my own Supreme Court, my own executive. . . . Rape was an insurrectionary act." Were you really being completely honest when you attributed your sexual attacks solely to ideological motives?

CLEAVER: Well, at that time, I'd read a smattering of revolutionary works, though not with very much understanding. Passionate things like Lenin's exhortatory writings, and Bakunin, and Nechayev's *Catechism of the Revolutionist.* And Machiavelli. I felt I knew what insurrection was and what rebellion was. So I called rape an insurrectionary act. But basically, it was my delight in violating what I conceived of as white men's laws, and my delight in defiling white women in revenge over the way white men have used black women. I was in a wild frame of mind and rape was simply one of the weird forms my rebellion took at that stage. So it was probably a combination of business and pleasure.

PLAYBOY: You went back to prison in 1958 for a fourteen-year sentence, after being convicted of assault with intent to kill and rape. During the nine years you served, what changed you to the point at which you admitted, in *Soul on Ice*, that you were wrong? "I had gone astray," you wrote, "astray not so much from the white man's law as from being human, civilized—for I could not approve the act of rape. Even though I had some insight into my own motivations, I did not feel justified. I lost my self-respect. My pride as a man dissolved and my whole fragile moral structure seemed to collapse, completely shattered."

CLEAVER: I came to realize that the particular women I had victimized had not been involved in actively oppressing me or other black people. I was taking revenge on them for what the whole system was responsible for. And as I thought about it, I felt I had become less than human. I also came to see that the price of hating other human beings is loving oneself less. But this didn't happen all at once; beginning to write was an important part of getting myself together. In fact, looking back, I started writing to save myself.

PLAYBOY: In none of your own writing so far have you gone into any detail about your formative years and about whether the pressures on you as a boy in the ghetto were representative, in your view, of the pressures on young black people throughout the society. Were they?

CLEAVER: So much so that I realized very soon after getting out of prison how little progress—if any—had been made in the nine years since I was sent up. What struck me more than anything else was the fact that the police still practice a systematic program to limit the opportunities in life for black cats by giving them a police record at an early age. In my own set, we were always being stopped and written up by the cops, even when we hadn't done anything. We'd just be walking down the street and the pigs would stop us and call in to see if we were wanted—all of which would serve to amass a file on us at headquarters. It's a general practice in this country that a young black gets put through this demeaning routine. But it's only one facet of the institutionalized conspiracy against black men in this country—to tame them, to break their spirit. As soon as he becomes aware of his environment, a black kid has to gauge his conduct and interpret his experiences in the context of his color and he has to orient himself to his environment in terms of how to survive as a black in a racist nation. But at least there's been one improvement in the years since I was a kid: Nowadays, being black— thanks to increasing white oppression—has been turned from a burden into an asset. Out there on the grade school and high school levels, young blacks are no longer uptight about their color. They're proud of it.

PLAYBOY: Among the manifestations of that new pride is a decline in social acceptability of the word "Negro" in favor of the terms "Afro-American" and "black." Is that why you don't call yourself or the Panthers "Negroes"?

CLEAVER: It's become a curse word because it has not only been of no use to black people but has prevented them from realizing the need to control their own institutions and to build their own sources of power. I mean, after all these years of talk about "integration," it hasn't meant a damn thing but more segregation and more powerlessness. "Integration" is a dead word now except insofar as you want to use it to stigmatize somebody—like I would say "Roy Wilkins, the integrationist."

PLAYBOY: W. H. Ferry of the Center for the Study of Democratic Institutions maintains that "integration does not seem likely in the United States now or in the future. Americans are afraid of living with differences." Do you agree?

CLEAVER: Well, talking about the future, I'd say that's up to white people. What black people want now is relief from being controlled and manipulated by white people. That could take the form of separation if white people continue to create conditions that make blacks convinced that total separation is the only alternative. If, on the other hand, conditions change sufficiently to end all exploitation and oppression of black people, then there is a possibility of integration in the long run for those who choose it. But we're a very long way from that.

PLAYBOY: In which direction would you like to see America go—toward separation or integration?

CLEAVER: Keeping in mind that we're talking about the very long view, it seems to me we're living in a world that has become virtually a neighborhood. If the world is not to destroy itself, the concept of people going their totally separate ways is really something that can't continue indefinitely. When you start speaking in ultimate terms, I don't see any way in which the world can be administered for the best interests of mankind without having a form of world government that would be responsive and responsible to *all* the people of the world—a world government that would function so that the welfare of no one segment of the population would be sacrificed for the enrichment of another.

PLAYBOY: How do you feel about Roy Wilkins' claim that America's black people really want what the white middle class already has under capitalism—split-level homes and all the accouterments of the affluent life?

CLEAVER: There's no question that black people want these things and have a right to them. The question is how to go about getting them. Many feel that they can get these things by entering into the mainstream of American society and becoming black capitalists. But to others, including myself, it's clear that in order for black people to have the best that society and technology are capable of providing, we need a new kind of society and a new kind of economic system. The goal must be to make possible a more equitable distribution of goods and services—but also to have a different set of values, so that things themselves don't become a substitute for life itself. In order to achieve that dual goal, we're going to have to move toward a new form of socialism. As long as there is so much stress on private property, we're going to have a society of competition rather than cooperation; we're going to have the exploited and the exploiters. Consider all these deeds, for example, that give people ownership of the productive and natural resources of this country. If there's going to be any burning, let's burn up these deeds, because everybody comes into this world the same way—naked, crying, without ownership of anything. The earth is here; it's given, like air and water, and I believe everyone should have equal access to its resources.

I want to see a society purged of Madison Avenue mind-benders who propagandize people into a mad pursuit of gadgets. They've conned people into believing that their lives depend on having an electric toothbrush, two cars and a color-television set in every room. We've got to rid ourselves of this dreadful and all-consuming hunger for *things,* this mindless substitution of the rat-race for a humane life. Only then will people become capable of relating to other people on the basis of individual merit, rather than on the basis of status, property and wealth. The values I'm for are really quite traditional and simple—like respecting your fellow man, respecting your parents, respecting your leaders if they're true leaders. These revolutionary goals are as old as time itself: Let people be. Let them fulfill their capacities.

PLAYBOY: The ultimate society you envision, in *Soul on Ice,* is one in which male and female will "realize their true nature," thereby closing the present "fissure of society into antagonistic classes" and regenerating "a dying culture and civilization alienated from its biology." But some critics of the book felt that you seemed to reserve this new Garden of Eden for black people, who, you claim, are "the wealth of a nation, an abundant supply of unexhausted, unde-essenced human raw material upon which the future of the society depends and with which, through the implacable march of history to an ever-broader base of democracy and equality, the society will renew and transform itself."

CLEAVER: No, it's not limited to black people. Black or white, the male-female principle is toward unity. Both black and white people have to get out of the bags they're in to be natural again. White people have to disabuse themselves of the illusion that it's their job to rule and that the black man's job is to produce labor. And black men have to use their minds and acquire confidence in the products of their minds. This doesn't mean the white man has to let *his* mind fall into disuse, but he also has to relate to his body again, as the black man does. What I'm saying is that everyone needs a new understanding of his total nature, mental and physical. Only when people, black and white, start seeing themselves and acting as total individuals, with bodies and minds, will they stop assigning exclusive mental roles to one set of people and exclusive physical roles to another. Only then will the primary thrust of life—the fusion of male and female—be freed of sociological obstacles. That's the base of the kind of social system I want to see, a society in which a man and a woman can come as close as possible to total unity on the basis of natural attraction. In my own life, the more totally I've been able to relate to a particular woman, the more fulfilled I've been.

PLAYBOY: Have you ever been tempted to withdraw from the front lines of the revolutionary social struggle to pursue that process of self-fulfillment in private life, by writing and raising a family with your wife Kathleen?

CLEAVER: I could do that. I could withdraw. I've got enough money from the book so that I could get myself a pad away from all this shit. I could go down to my parole officer and say, "Look, man, I don't want to go back to prison. I'm going to stop talking revolution. I'm going to start writing poetry and fairy tales

the way you want me to and I won't be a problem anymore. So how about re-evaluating my case and leaving
me alone? Live and let live." I know they'd go for that,
and I wouldn't need much money to do it, because I'm
not hung up on material things. But the fact is that I
feel *good* working with my people and with the brothers
of the Black Panther Party. I'd feel miserable doing
anything else. Hell, most of my life has been involved
in conflicts with authority, and now that I've politicized
that conflict, I'm very content to be working for black
liberation. I couldn't conceive of myself playing any
other role—not even if I have to go back to prison for
it. I'm going to do everything I can *not* to go back to
prison, but I can't compromise my beliefs. I'd rather
be dead than do that. And I may have a violent end,
anyway. I'm hearing more and more these days from
people telling me to be careful, because they feel my
life's in danger. They may be right, but I say fuck it.

PLAYBOY: If you are imprisoned or killed, how much
confidence do you have that the Black Panther Party or
any succeeding group in the revolutionary struggle will
ultimately prevail?

CLEAVER: I have confidence that people learn from
experiences of others. Every time a black man is murdered for speaking out against oppression, his death is
fuel for the struggle to continue. When Malcolm was
killed, that didn't frighten people; his death created
more disciples. I can only hope that if what I'm doing
has any constructive value, others will take up the fight
and continue it if I'm killed. Che Guevara put it the
way I feel, when he said: "Wherever death may surprise us, let it be welcome, provided that this, our battle
cry, may have reached some receptive ear and another

hand may be extended to wield our weapons." That's all I ask for.

PLAYBOY: How do you rate your chances of survival?

CLEAVER: I plan to be around for quite a while.

October, 1968

Acknowledgments

*The editor wishes to thank John J. Simon of Random House
and Peter Collier of* Ramparts *who, in a real sense, co-edited
the book with me. I want to express my gratitude to Kathleen Cleaver, Anne Weills Scheer and David Kolodney
who found the time to read the manuscript and to help
straighten out the introduction. Thanks are also due to Kate
Gilpin, Cathy Stone, Jane C. Seitz, Anne Dowie, Sandra
Levinson, Margaret Wolfe, Elizabeth Dore, Robb Cunning-
ham, Jan Austin, Berenice Hoffman, Cicely Nichols, Leslie
Timan, and Cordelia Jason who helped in the preparation
of the manuscript for the printer.*

*Steve Baron, Random House production manager and
David Seaman were responsible for the book's rapid and
effective manufacture. Carl Weiss and Cynthia Krupat are to
be thanked for their contribution to its design.*

*Finally there would not be a book were it not for the
dedication, advice, and persistent good taste of Cyrilly Abels,
Eldridge Cleaver's literary agent.*

*I remain, of course, responsible for the collection offered
here.*

R.S.

Schultz